DEAD RECKONINGS

A Review of Horror and the Weird in the Arts
Edited by Alex Houstoun and Michael J. Abolafia

No. 27 (Spring 2020)

3   Go Buy *Black Heart Boys' Choir:* A Review and Comparative Reading ....Géza A. G. Reilly
    Curtis M. Lawson, *Black Heart Boys' Choir*.

7   Epistemological Alchemy .... Michael D. Miller
    Matt Cardin, *To Rouse Leviathan*.

16 The Return of the Fanzine .... S. T. Joshi
    Obadiah Baird, ed. *The Audient Void*; David Barker, *Half in Light, Half in Shadow*; Graeme Phillips, ed. *Cyäegha*.

25 Ramsey's Rant: Just a Coincidence .... Ramsey Campbell

29 The Dark Gnosis of D. L. Myers................ Leigh Blackmore
    D. L. Myers, *Oracles from the Black Pool*.

32 More "Thing" .... Darrell Schweitzer
    John W. Campbell, Jr., *Frozen Hell,* ed. John Gregory Betancourt.

36 Polluting Gods: Liminality, Devolution, and the Defamiliarization of Human Identity in Blackwood's "The Wendigo" and Kipling's "The Mark of the Beast" ....
    Michael J. Abolafia

48 Unseen Worlds, Waiting to Be Discovered... Daniel Pietersen
    Melissa Edmundson, ed. *Women's Weird: Strange Stories by Women*

51 A Trade in Futures .... Daniel Raskin

55 Dare You Have Fun?................................Fiona Maeve Geist
    Nick Mamatas, *Sabbath*.

58 Dying to Meet You ....Karen Joan Kohoutek
    Playghoul: Special Vampira Issue.

61 The Nature of Horror .... S. T. Joshi
    Ramsey Campbell, *The Wise Friend*.

65 Wisdom in Anguish: Sloane Leong's Dysmorphic Space Mechs .... Helen Chazan
Sloane Leong, *With the Blade as Witness.*

69 Australia's Weird Poet Laureate .... Leigh Blackmore
Kyla Lee Ward, *The Macabre Modern and Other Morbidities.*

71 An Historical and Environmental Reading of August Derleth's "Ithaqua" .... Edward Guimont

82 Cosmic Horror—with a Dash of Sex .... Gary Fry
S. T. Joshi, *Something from Below.*

84 Providentially Speaking Again .... Donald Sidney-Fryer
T. E. D. Klein, *Providence After Dark and Other Writings.*

89 *Some of Your Blood:* Dracula's Metafictional Mirror ....
Philip Challinor

95 About the Contributors

DEAD RECKONINGS is published by Hippocampus Press, P.O. Box 641, New York, NY 10156 (www.hippocampuspress.com). Copyright © 2020 by Hippocampus Press. Cover art by Jason C. Eckhardt. Cover design by Barbara Briggs Silbert. Hippocampus Press logo by Anastasia Damianakos. Orders and subscriptions should be sent to Hippocampus Press. Contact Alex Houstoun at deadreckoningsjournal@gmail.com for assignments or before submitting a publication for review.

ISSN 1935-6110   ISBN 978-1-61498-300-2

Go Buy *Black Heart Boys' Choir:* A Review and Comparative Reading

Géza A. G. Reilly

CURTIS M. LAWSON. *Black Heart Boys' Choir.* n.p.: Wyrd Horror, 2019. 241 pp. $14.99 tpb. ISBN: 978-1-0751-0806-8.

Every fan of horror and the weird should go out and read Curtis M. Lawson's *Black Heart Boys' Choir.* The novel is well paced, exquisitely plotted, and exceptionally well written. Although the novel reads almost like a young-adult horror story at first, it quickly reveals itself to be a rather brutal and mature affair. Its protagonist, Lucien Beaumont, is realistically crafted, and his first-person narration is meticulously composed. The novel is a treat in every way, and it has one of the most brilliantly executed climaxes I've ever come across in a horror narrative. The single flaw I could find in the book (the strained way in which the eponymous choir got its name) does not come close to outweighing its virtues. This is a novel well worth your time.

Now that the frontloading is done, let's talk about *Black Heart Boys' Choir* in relation to two other novels that came out recently: David Peak's *Corpsepaint* (Word Horde, 2018) and Grady Hendrix's *We Sold Our Souls* (Quirk Books, 2018). Let's stack the basics next to each other first. *Black Heart Boys' Choir* concerns Lucien Beaumont, who, driven by love of music and reverence for his recently deceased father, who worked as a composer, establishes a choir at the public school he has been forced to attend due to his family's diminished means. The choir, composed of misfits and outsiders, begins recomposing *Madrigal of the World's End,* Lucien's father's final work, leading to sinister events before and during their ultimate performance. *Corpsepaint* is the story of Roland and Max, two black metal musicians (the former stalled as an up-and-comer and the latter fading as a star whose best work was decades prior) who become embroiled in a cosmic-horror plot by working on an album with The Wisdom of Silenus, a band and a fringe community in the Ukraine. *We Sold Our Souls* focuses on Kris Pulaski, a formerly popular heavy metal guitarist who is now down on her luck, and her struggle to save the world from demonic forces that have infected her old band.

What fascinates me about *Black Heart Boys' Choir* in light of these other two novels is what it has to say about talent and the presumption of greatness. Lucien has a passion for music, yes, but he is not a naturally talented guitarist like Kris; he is not an innovator like Max; he is not immersed in the art of translating human experience of the world into music like Roland. And yet, throughout the novel Lucien claims to be a musical genius. There is no demonstrative reason to agree that Lucien is more talented than the average high school glee-club member, and yet these flaws in Lucien's thought are brushed away magnificently by the arrogance of this actually rather ordinary young man. Indeed, the reader of *Black Heart Boys' Choir* can almost be hypnotized by Lucien's narration (as several characters are duped by his dialogue and bearing) if they do not stop to winnow out the truth from Lucien's persistent web of self-delusion and aggrandizement.

Lucien never bothers to entertain doubts about his talent because he is convinced that he is one of the great; he is only lost amidst a sea of the mediocre. This is not a delusion that Max or Roland are prone to: they both come from humble roots at best, and they are nihilistically convinced that having come from nothing, they will return to nothing. Their ambition toward creating music that will speak for and outlive them is a fool's errand in their eyes, even if they are driven to accomplish it. And Kris, who has already achieved greatness by the standards of her profession, has discovered by the time of the start of the novel how easily someone can be brought low. Lucien, however, consistently complains that he, being one of the great, is in peril of being torn down by the small. As said, however, this is a delusion, because Lucien does not create anything at all. His greatness is all surface-level: he is the child of a composer who may have been great (Lucien's account is biased, of course), he evidences a modicum of self-discipline in his personal appearance, he happens to have good taste in classical music, and he has dedicated himself to performing a score written by someone else. He produces *nothing* original and has done *nothing* worthy of counting himself among the great. And yet, Lucien's self-delusion is so powerful that when it is voiced, he leaves characters who know better at a loss for a response. This, in turn, is a way to fiendishly play into the imp of the perverse present in those readers who have at one time or another been tempted to think of themselves as being great—if only they were not held back by the small.

These elements, and the masterful composition deployed here, are what set Lawson's novel apart from Hendrix's and Peak's narratives. Ultimately, *Black Heart Boys' Choir* is less about demonic forces co-opting talented musicians, qua Hendrix, and it is less about the struggle of creation against cosmic indifference, qua Peak. Rather, it approaches the almost-subgenre of music-themed horror by making the site of investigation and fear the idea of self-perception and self-identification. The existence of *Madrigal of the World's End* is, really, a McGuffin designed to allow the reader to work out what is really at issue here: the horror of how someone might be so wrong about himself and the world around him, and the terrible consequences that might arise as a result of those misjudgments.

I am loath to use a cliché like "this is a timely novel," but in the case of *Black Heart Boys' Choir* the cliché fits. We live in an era when the dangers of not understanding ourselves and the points of intersection between ourselves and others are monstrously easy to fall prey to. Certainly, any one of us can think of innumerable examples of people being incapable of self-reflection, and if we should fall short, the nightly news has more than enough evidence for us to dwell on. The technologies that many of us, myself included, use on a daily basis seem to foster this ignorance of ourselves and our relation to others, easing the birth of so many terrible events. With Lucien, *Black Heart Boys' Choir* forces the reader to confront a stunning example of just such an ignorant person and, as all great novels do, think about the fabric of our own lives.

For while *We Sold Our Souls* ends on a slightly downbeat

but nevertheless hopeful note, and *Corpsepaint* ends with a nihilistic, ineffective thud, *Black Heart Boys' Choir* ends with a crescendo that is as close to perfect as it can come. Indeed, it ends as Lucien lived: masterfully composed, confused, and ultimately pointless. Out of the three novels mentioned here, I was most struck by the end of Lawson's effort simply because it forces us to wonder about the great and the small and how these dichotomies are as fragile as gossamer in a winter wind. There is no hope here of the great rising to replace the great, or that art's meaning will endure past our end. There is only the warning that believing ourselves great or talented is *not enough to be great or talented*. We must, instead, not just do the work of our *art* but do the work of *ourselves* as well. We must, unlike Lucien, know who we are and not rest on the trappings we inherit or scavenge from others. We must, instead, strive for an awareness of ourselves and others that can build all of us up, for the alternative is only an arrogant pose of self-reinforcement that, in the end, threatens to tear everything down.

Epistemological Alchemy

Michael D. Miller

MATT CARDIN. *To Rouse Leviathan*. New York: Hippocampus Press, 2019. 376 pp. $20.00 tpb. ISBN: 978-1-61498-270-8

Magnum Opus! The term distinguishes a literary or artistic masterpiece, specifically an artist's greatest work. So what does this have to do with this substantial volume of Matt Cardin's work? Within the confines of *To Rouse Leviathan* coils a collection of philosophical-religious horror spanning a period of twenty years. Taken as a whole, this may indeed be such a magnum opus if you find academic delivery of cosmic horror and weirdness to be so rarely offered, for this collection delivers with all the intensity of Nietzsche's philosophical hammer wielded by H. P. Lovecraft and Thomas Ligotti.

Critically and academically speaking, this collection of stories allows one to put philosophical criticism to the test. A more recent literary theory on the far side of reader response, deconstruction, or intersectional analysis, philosophical criticism may best be summed up the belief as all writers (and artists) have a viewpoint, a philosophical outlook that is the engine of every story (or art). Stories would succeed or fail when delivering that viewpoint. My first exposure to this theory was in S. T. Joshi's *The Weird Tale* (1990), where weird fiction was expressed as "the consequence of a worldview," and it encompasses Cardin's theme incarnate.

Before we proceed with the stories, what exactly is this theme? To make the exigence easily comprehensible on a surface level, take Lovecraftian cosmicism (the natural state of humanity as complete alienation from an indifferent universe) and conjoin the author's personal religious upbringing and scholarly pursuits. This may seem like an odd pairing, so a little elucidation is due.

In the work's preface Cardin explains the concept of "the

void" existing before God in Hebrew scripture, then links the similarities of definition to Sumerian *Tiamat* and then Babylonian primeval chaos establishing that this "void" is the true reality of the universe and God is a temporary condition fighting against this truth. So here is the basis for the merging of cosmicism with a religious context. Cardin gives a hint of this throughout the collection in a series of epigraphs that precede each part or chapter, and they run the gamut from Lovecraft to Robert Frost, Rudolf Otto, Shakespeare, William James, and heavily biblical quotations from Ecclesiastes, Genesis, Job, and Psalms. This is taken a step further by adding Ligotti-esque insights on the universe and the human condition. This void is the only true reality holding "the seams of the universe" and is revealed when attempting to "divine the deep." There you have it. A Lovecraftian/Ligottian universe with divinity. On to the stories.

Part One: Divinations of the Deep

The opening narrative, "An Abhorrence to All Flesh," establishes the standard trope character of these stories—usually a religious academic with a "smattering of knowledge from many different fields of inquiry" and a self-confessed bibliophile. These characters then attempt to "divine the deep." In this case, Todd Whitman is invited to an old college friend's (Darby Cole) estate learning of his colleague's familial curse going back to Egypt and a chance meeting with an ancient priest of "The Temple of Jehovah" seeking Whitman's historical validation. The temple of course is dedicated to exposing the truth about God and his second-place standing in the universe after the void. During several exchanges of religious knowledge Whitman departs and is plagued by dreams revealing that "the truth is hidden in the flesh." Whitman later confronts Darby Cole for further elucidation and matches the philosophy of "The Temple of Jehovah" to biblical book of Numbers, quoting verse:

> "And they shall go forth, and look upon the carcasses of the men that have transgressed against me: for their worm shall

not die, neither shall their fire be quenched: and they shall be an abhorring unto all flesh."

Whitman spends the night trying to piece the theology together, but not before being disturbed by Darby Cole screaming as he is consumed by his ancestral curse, the void reaching through and immolating his flesh. Whitman flees the manse and weeks later is reduced to a Young Goodman Brown type figure, a victim of theological horror, whose finals words are: "I could no longer lie . . . My columns, my reviews, my essays, were now impossible, for I found that I could write nothing but words and phrases appropriate for a madman's diary."

"Notes of a Mad Copyist" continues the theological horror, this time set in the appropriate Abbey of Mont-Saint-Michel during the Middle Ages. Here the monk-scribe protagonist copies out the word of God "according to the outline of the Divine Office." It is not very long before "the vision of the world as a kind of empty shell, congealed around a core of nothingness" begins to scroll out on the monk's pages resulting in his imprisonment and ultimate trial for his final screed:

> Our Grandfathers who art in chaos
> Fallow by they names
> The kingdom scour, They will devour
> The earth, and hell, and heaven.

"The Basement Theater" is a short, almost absurdist work where the unknown narrator is invited to a play in an abandoned theater, only to find himself becoming part of the drama that acts out his death over and over in eternal paradox. While the story is short on substance it is remarkable for where it starts. All Cardin's stories choose to start far into the conflict, where we feel as if we cannot get out. The narrator is already looking at the faded marquee of the theater as he steps into the ruins in the opening sentence. What's going happen? This expectation is vividly set up with every story in the volume.

"If It Had Eyes" is another similar excursion. This time the narrator wanders around a strange city with place names such as Malvent Hill and Simon's Cathedral as a murky fog follows him. Religious iconography is used in descriptions referencing

"The Harrowing of Hell" as our narrator and fog become conscious of each other. The story has the tone and feel of Lovecraft's "The Festival" with its dreamlike climax and the fog's revelation to the narrator of "measureless caverns, a submarine kingdom whose secrets form the very foundation of the world."

"Judas of the Infinite" provides quite the climactic reversal as the Mad Copyist has returned to our modern world seeking out the downtrodden and showing the true reality of universe as carrying out the true purpose of God. In this story the thematic element takes form as actual action: uncreation. Here it's revealed that creation is the work of God as a bulwark to hide the void, the truth of that is revealed through uncreation, undoing the creation of God—or so it seems.

Part Two: Dark Awakenings

The mid-section of the volume contains some of the best work. In "Teeth" we have two philosophy graduate students, Jason and Marco, in the last years of writing dissertations. Marco of course is the more maddening of the two, who believes he's on to the true nature of the universe. In this theory the void is an almost physical incarnation with a set of reality-devouring teeth. Jason might be a stand-in for the author's personal experiences—"Teaching philosophy to uninterested freshmen is a bit like asking your cat to come to you. They really don't give a shit." Marco shares his notebooks with Jason, who reads them one evening trying to parcel together an insane treatise on quantum mechanics, religion, philosophy, and H. P. Lovecraft. In sum, the work exposes a "a dark emanation" as the core of life and "the human need for illusion" to conceal it.

That night Jason dreams of a vortex lined with teeth that nearly consumes him before he awakes from the nightmare. Not surprisingly, Marco has plans to put this into action by eliminating a rival philosopher/astrologist they both appreciate, Nigel Williamson, presently in town for a lecture. While this story is a heavy-handed exploration of major philosophies and scientific theories that can be exhaustive, the climax is unforgettable, as Jason arrives at the lecture too late, finding

Marcos as the teeth, digesting Nigel Williamson like an intellectual hors d'oeuvre down "the bottomless throat of a cosmic mystery that forever feeds on all things." The climax employs the post-narrative confession trope, with Jason talking to someone, perhaps in a psych ward, converted to the philosophy of the void—"to exist at all is to know the horror of no escape." With this story the volume as shifts into a more Ligotti-style dirge against meaning as the remaining stories bear out.

"The Stars Shine without Me" is futuristic *Brazil*-like tour of Viggo Brand and the Brand Corporation. Our protagonist/narrator, after working his way through the meaningless universe as a Brand corporation employee who does nothing but fail at his tasks, finds himself invited to speak with Mr. Brand. The story is an almost absurdist reversal of the Melville classic "Bartleby the Scrivener," this time reimagined as weird fiction. The protagonist is rewarded for his actions of doing nothing and his notes on the dreary existence of everyday life. Brand shares with him the purpose of his corporation, popping up in city after city, sucking out the lifeblood of their inhabitants. The story is an interesting attack on corporate business models and has an eerie semblance to *Phantasm*: there is a mortuary service visiting town after town, and Kubrick's *2001: A Space Odyssey* as our protagonist sees the true work of the Brand corporation as a final cosmic vision that spans the spiral arms of the galaxy.

"Desert Places" is an interesting divergence into modern horror, one of the most well-written of the stories centered on a love triangle between very humanized characters that spans many years. However, the forlorn love interest of the protagonist is only concerned with stealing life energy for her dying partner. Not too obviously emphasizing the theme of *To Rouse Leviathan,* the story still packs plenty of religious and philosophical allusions meriting a place in the volume.

"Blackbrain Dwarf" is one of the purer horror bloodbaths in the collection. This time Derek, a failing lawyer, locked in a loveless marriage to Linda, is slowly corrupted by a "dark emanation" taking over his mind. Derek senses this as a "wrongness." The emanation is described as a blackbrain dwarf . . . "a bloodthirsty Dwarf crouched low in the dark, and he carried in his huge hand the pulsing feather of vengeance, plucked from the bloodangel's wing." (One can't help but see another *Phantasm* connection here in the dwarf-like servitors of the alien mortician, the Tall Man.) When the emanation takes over, violence and mayhem ensue, instigated first by Derek catching Linda in bed with another man. It is ultimately a visceral depiction of the incursion of weirdness.

"The Devil and One Lump" is our divine comedic break in the collection, a story of the writing process as catharsis in one part, and a battle of wills between the narrator and the Devil over "total cognitive annihilation." Throughout the collection we sense many possible autobiographical interludes, yet this story has some of the more obvious aphorisms. "I woke up that morning and stepped right into a story that I might have written—back when I could still write, that is. And even then, I only would have written such as story if I were a hack who dealt in shameless clichés instead of a serious student of the dark self." Or, "Horror novels are one thing, but religious horror novels—or horrific religious novels, if you prefer—are quite another." The story at its crux contains the core iteration of "the consequence of a worldview." As the Devil relates genuine Matt Cardin for us:

> You have taken the entire Christian cosmology and, more importantly, and the characteristic tenor of those who call themselves Christians, and you have turned those on their head. You have speculated that the Bible contains a hidden subtext . . . You have written of a narcissistic demiurge that represses the memory of his birth from a monstrous prior reality . . . You've launched an assault on the deepest philosophical and theological foundations . . .

There you have it. The battle of this story is reveled to be who is the best at self-deception.

"The God of Foulness" finishes the section as its standout tale, even more so if read during (and after) the Covid-19 outbreak of 2020. The premise of the story is a cult named "The Sick Seekers" that intentionally catches and spreads disease. It is not hard to feel the ominous threat of that plot device, getting its inspiration from the *Necronomicon*—"As a foulness shall ye know them." The formula is quite simple. Our narrator, a writer for the *Terence Sun-Gazette*, is assigned to research and write a story on the cult. Though the process of covering the story the narrator catches a disease, is invited to join the cult, and learns that disease is how "the god" communicates the true nature of the universe—we should want to get sick, to embrace it. The cult of course has a ritual where disease is exchanged from themselves to a summoned entity that is a physical manifestation of the void. On a deeper level, as the protagonist makes the journey into the world of the Sick Seekers he still wrestles with his mother's death to cancer, as if by going through this ordeal he can obtain peace with her memory. As for the climax we have another Young Goodman Brown moment as the narrator discovers there are encampments of the Sick Seekers cult all over the world. "They are spreading their gospel of disease, and I cannot doubt but that their ranks will grow even faster as people discover the freedom from suffering that waits them in the embrace of the God." One can think of such scenarios during epidemics and quarantines where citizens do not follow recommendations or stay-at-home orders. It is one of the best stories in the collection asking tough questions. "What does it matter whether the body, or even the mind or soul, is replaced by a facsimile?" The disease is revealed to be "individual selfhood—the last and truest disease."

Part III: Apocryphon

The third and final section hones and compresses most of the theological discourse into some tight narratives. "Chimeras & Grotesqueries: An Unfinished Fragment of A Daemonic Derangement" is Cardin's entry in the hoax-book trope, this one written by one Philip Lasine. The book is found and introduced by another religious scholar/semi-autobiographical narrator and tells the story of a homeless man through whose point of view we see the world in an entirely different connotation. Though a character already alienated and removed from life, he becomes the perfect catalyst for watching the apocalypse. The apocalypse is "mass hysteria" described as "hallucinatory disfiguration." The homeless narrator describes the hysteria on his daily and nightly wandering from his hole in the side of a building. While the hysteria smites the minds of the urban populace, the narrator experiences memories of his former life. The manuscript is unfinished, but as a narrative it towers above the other stories in carrying out its Ligotti theme: "the godhead is insane, and the supernatural is its insanity." True to the unity of this collection, the manuscript was found lying on the front porch of an abandoned Methodist rectory.

"Prometheus Possessed" is an odd interlude into the future, a Sci-Fi Papacy of sorts set in a "Ringworld"-like setting, except that this one is administered by clergy. The story is a heavy-handed barrage of specialized terminology, by far the least impressive of the collection, but is convincing in building a world crossed with *1984* and a nightmare Christian version of Scientology. The basic conflict revolves around the Ministry of Psychic Sanitation discovering a "dark substance" creating a heavily "diseased reality." It's a tale of trying to cast out sickness only to find the result begets only more.

"The New Pauline Corpus" finishes out the work. Back to the mode of long philosophical exchanges between characters, this story analyzes writing itself and its place as an attempt to understand our lives on this planet. The perspective is Judeo-Christian, the conflict is between the "reverence for a good story" (as the final episode of *Game of Thrones* tried to emphasize) and a war between "levels of reality." Here again we revisit the theme of uncreation and with references to Lovecraftian lore, attempting to make the story a part of that mythos. The narrator gives a set of insights to his audience, one named Francis, while descriptive passages of walking through the cataclysmic end of the world break off the narrative. The insights are tied to various forces both religious, cosmic, and Lovecraftian: Omnipresence (Yog-Sothoth and Azathoth), Annihilating Holiness (Yahweh, Luther, Moses), Transcendence (Book of Isaiah), Awefulness (New Testament, Tiamat), Immanence (Jerusalem and R'lyeh). These insights are part of the narrator's treatise, a self-described "third testament" that explains "what has Christ to do with Cthulhu?"

Not so much a story as a meta-fiction, it coalesces the entirety of the collection into a clear principled philosophical discourse into primal mystery.

Admittedly, the rigor of these stories may not be for every searcher after horror, but Cardin's style compensates for the scholarly academics with fluid and appropriate simplicity. The narratives are rife with figurative language, with some standout moments: "The house, which squatted sphinxlike under the starry firmament"; "It seemed as if the wind were determined to scoop the entire monastery up from its precarious perch on the mountain shelf and hurl us to a craggy death"; and "as if an interior network of branching corridors in my soul had been demolished and buried beneath a mountain of dead earth."

To Rouse Leviathan is a thinking person's literary tour of cosmic horror. It is about ideas that do not fade after reading. Its place in the oeuvre of weird literature is warranted. It is Ligotti's *The Conspiracy against the Human Race* put into literary fiction. It is the cosmic Gospel according to St. Cardin.

The Return of the Fanzine

S. T. Joshi

OBADIAH BAIRD, ed. *The Audient Void*. Numbers 6 (2018), 7 (2019), and 8 (2019). [Salem, OR:] Audient Void Publishing. 54 pp. each. No ISBN. $8.00 per issue.
DAVID BARKER. *Half in Light, Half in Shadow*. [Salem, OR:] Audient Void Publishing, 2019. 52 pp. No ISBN. $12.00 chapbook (signed/numbered).
GRAEME PHILLIPS, ed. *Cyäegha*. Numbers 20 (Summer 2018; 48 pp.), 21 (Summer 2019; 40 pp.), and 22 (Autumn 2019, 44 pp.). No ISBN. £4.00 (plus postage). Limited to 75 copies.

In the field of weird fiction, the first fanzine of any consequence was the *Fantasy Fan* (1933–35), whose eighteen monthly issues were edited by the very young Charles D. Hornig (1916–1999). This was a typeset journal (the typesetting and printing were done by Conrad Ruppert), and in spite of its occasional crudities in design, was a splendid vehicle that allowed devotees of Lovecraft, Clark Ashton Smith, and *Weird Tales* to congregate in print. Incredibly, it obtained contributions from Lovecraft, Smith, and even the relentlessly professional Robert E. Howard and August Derleth, along with the usual array of fan articles, news notes, and so on. It made the regrettable decision to initiate a deliberately provocative column, "The Boiling Point," in which Forrest J Ackerman levied a harsh attack on Clark Ashton Smith, leading to furious responses over the next several issues until the column was finally curtailed; but otherwise, it served a vital function in fostering interest in the genre.[1]

Science fiction and fantasy developed its own fanzines at roughly the same period, among them *Fantasy Magazine* (ed. Julius Schwartz), the *Phantagraph* (ed. Donald A. Wollheim),

---

1. See the facsimile reprint, *The Fantasy Fan* (Lance Thingmaker, 2010).

and the *Science-Fantasy Correspondent* (ed. Willis Conover). Some of these lasted for only a few issues, but they were often begun by writers and editors who would later on become distinguished in their fields: the young James Blish coedited a few issues of the *Planeteer,* and Ray Bradbury launched a fanzine, *Futuria Fantasia,* that ran for four issues in 1939–40.[2] More specifically in the realm of weird fiction, R. H. Barlow edited two substantial issues of *Leaves* (1937–38).[3] Shortly thereafter, Francis T. Laney and others began the *Acolyte* (1942–46), one of the most notable fanzines specifically devoted to Lovecraft. I say "notable" only in terms of its contents; its first issue, run off on ditto, is now virtually illegible, and its subsequent issues (reproduced by mimeograph) are not a great deal better. But it too served as a forum for the growing Lovecraft fandom movement, soliciting contributions (even if in some cases they were only letters or short commentary) by Robert Bloch, E. Hoffmann Price, Professor T. O. Mabbott, and many others.

The *Acolyte* did not publish a great deal of fiction, and subsequent fanzines continued to focus on criticism, such as *Haunted* (1963–68; ed. Samuel D. Russell), *Shadow* (1968–74; ed. David A. Sutton), and *Nyctalops* (1970–91; ed. Harry O. Morris, Jr.). Some of these magazines did begin publishing noteworthy fiction later in their runs. *Nyctalops* will be forever cherished for providing a forum for the early tales of Thomas Ligotti, as well as for publishing his first book, *Songs of a Dead Dreamer* (1986), under Morris's book imprint, Silver Scarab Press, and *Whispers* (1973–87; ed. Stuart David Schiff) published fiction by Stephen King and other bestselling authors at a fairly early stage.

In the 1970s, two amateur press associations—adapting the methods of the two leading old-time amateur journalism organizations, the National Amateur Press Association (founded in 1876) and the United Amateur Press Association

---

2. There is a facsimile reprint, *Futuria Fantasia* (Graham Publishing, 2007).

3. I have recently prepared a reset reprint, also including an amateur journal, *The Dragon-Fly,* that Barlow edited in 1935–36: *The Dragon-Fly and Leaves* (Sarnath Press, 2020).

(founded in 1895)—emerged. REHUPA (Robert E. Howard United Press Association) began in 1972, and the Esoteric Order of Dagon (devoted to the study of H. P. Lovecraft) began in 1973. Both associations are still going, although their publications, with rare exceptions, are quite humble in appearance. But *Crypt of Cthulhu* (1981f.; ed. Robert M. Price) began as a contribution to the EOD, and Graeme Phillips's *Cyäegha* is still sent through the EOD.

Which brings us to the two fanzines under review here. It is unjust even to refer to them as "fanzines," for their overall design and contents lift them far above the frequently pejorative connotation of that term. Certainly, the computer has made it far easier to prepare a "zine" that looks as distinguished as any journal that claims to be fully professional, and technology has also facilitated the printing of such zines so that they don't look as if they emerged from the printing press of a teenager.

Obadiah Baird, whose impressive beard gives him something of the appearance of a biblical patriarch, is still a relatively young man who runs a bookstore in Salem, Oregon. He began *The Audient Void* (the title is derived from the memorable first paragraph of Lovecraft's prose poem "Nyarlathotep": "Nyarlathotep . . . the crawling chaos . . . I am the last . . . I will tell the audient void") in 2016. I remember seeing an early issue at the home of the late W. H. Pugmire and being immediately impressed—but also touched by this deliberate throwback, whose heyday I still remember fondly (I have been Official Editor of the EOD for more than thirty years). In the editorial of his eighth issue, Baird is refreshingly candid about his self-doubts about his editorial capacities ("I have no business editing a magazine"); but he goes on to point out that even Lovecraft, Smith, and others were similarly beset with self-doubts about the merits of their work, so there is no reason why Baird shouldn't continue his work. And he has every reason to do so.

The Audient Void is an engaging mix of fiction, poetry, and commentary—although the last feature is restricted to Baird's own editorials and to David Barker's "Ye Olde Lemurian," a column that evidently began in the mid-1990s when it appeared in *Midnight Shambler* (then edited by Robert M. Price). Barker's column is eminently readable and informative. In issue 6 he recounts his meetings with the fantasy writer John Eric Holmes, whose extensive book collection Barker was lucky enough to glimpse; in issue 7 he tells of his several trips to Hawaii and delves into possible parallels between the gods of the old Hawaiian religion and those of the Cthulhu Mythos (these parallels are probably fanciful, since Lovecraft is fairly clear that he derived the overall concept of the Mythos from the work of Lord Dunsany, with input by Arthur Machen and others); and in issue 8 Barker writes a lengthy and moving tribute to his friend W. H. Pugmire and spells out the details of his three collaborative volumes with Pugmire.

But the bulk of *The Audient Void* is devoted to fiction. Fanzines traditionally have a difficult time attracting top-flight authors, for the simple reason that they either do not pay or pay fairly low rates; but in these days, when there are relatively few paying magazines in the weird field (the original anthology has largely replaced the magazine as a venue for professional writers), Baird has been able to fill his journal with at least a few notable names. And yet, it is clear that he is devoted to finding new talent and showcasing their work, under the admirable (and sensible) premise that there is an enormous amount of excellent work out there and not a great many places where it can appear. Hence, in issue 6 all three contributors of short stories are making their first appearance in print here. I cannot in truth say that these stories are absolutely stellar, but they are certainly of interest. Michael Gray Baughan's "The Children of Euphonia" is a somewhat mystifying steampunk story about a woman overwhelmed by a machine. Chris Kuriata's "Things to Save in a Fire" is a brooding narrative about an old woman (who may have been a witch and also a prostitute in her earlier life) deciding what to save when her house catches on fire; she chooses the bones of a boy whom she had killed some years before. Josh Reynolds, in "Bruno J. Lampini and the Boots of Frankenstein," writes a story of rollicking humor and lively narrative drive whose deliberately preposterous premise somehow compels the reader to keep on reading.

The stories in issue 7 are quite a bit better; indeed, Nicole Vasari's "On Midsummer" is an exquisite horror/fantasy hybrid, even though the exact progression of its plot is at times opaque. The basic thrust of the story is a girl's desire to resurrect her dead brother, Robin, and she manages to accomplish the deed, but with unexpected results. What is remarkable about this story is its flawlessly musical prose:

> Then there was an awful piercing sound of glass shattering but amplified beyond endurance. A seam shimmered and trembled in the air, a crack of light, thrashing in and out of existence. Beyond that, if she had looked, was the door to the endless summer country of the blest where the gods lived in their far wasteland. And the last of Robin Gower's human soul flew into the flame.

That is worthy of Lord Dunsany—and the story bears further relations to Dunsany, especially in the fusion of the human and natural worlds, a central theme in the work of the Anglo-Irish writer. The two other stories in the issue are not quite as notable. "The Salt Witch" by dave ring [*sic*] has an awkward transition from second-person to first-person narration, but does feature a grim and powerful ending. But "The Arkham Express" by Don Webb and Glynn Owen Barrass is a disappointment, in spite of the fact that the authors are widely published professionals. The story (mercifully) is not a Lovecraftian tale, but one about a man who finds a train set that his father had given to him as a boy and who manages to enter the world of the train set. The tale is, I fear, inane and directionless, and also marred by solecisms and execrable punctuation.

Issue 8 finds Josh Reynolds returning with another narrative about Bruno J. Lampini—perhaps not quite as engaging as its predecessor, but lively and clever enough. Cynthia Ward's "Midnight in the Oasis of Mahrah" is a compelling story of two young women in a fantasy realm attacked by "reavers" but who summon supernatural powers to prevail. S. L. Edwards's "Pulses: A Second-Life Story," written in second-person narration, is a powerfully moving account of the resurrected dead.

Poetry fills the magazine from beginning to end; indeed,

Baird strikingly admits in his editorial in issue 8 that "I view poetry as the backbone of *The Audient Void*." He has certainly featured some of the best weird poets writing today: Ann K. Schwader (here collaborating with David C. Kopaska-Merkel), K. A. Opperman, Adam Bolivar, Ashley Dioses, D. F. Myers. and several others, including such occasional poets as John Shirley and Nicole Cushing. But Baird commits the gaffe of presenting almost all the poems *with lines centered across the page*. He surely knows this is not how poetry is or should be laid out; I know for a fact that these same poets (who also submit to my weird poetry journal, *Spectral Realms*) do not submit their poems in this manner. It may be easier to format this way, but it seriously disfigures the poems and falsifies the reading experience. He does deign to print ballads (written in quatrains) by Bolivar and Chelsea Arrington in the orthodox manner; but he would be well advised to print all the other poems similarly. The problem does not affect prose poems such as Maxwell I. Gold's "Cyber Things," which chillingly focuses (as much of his work does) on the horrific potential of our subjugation to technology, here represented by the smartphone.

In issue 6 Baird's editorial extends lavish and deserved praise to Dan Sauer, who wears numerous hats for the magazine (the masthead credits him with "Graphic Design / Layout / Copyediting / Illustration"). The illustrations in all three issues, many of them collages, merit particular commendation for their grim evocativeness. But it's possible that Sauer is wearing a few too many hats, as there are occasional copyediting slips ("compliment" for "complement" [on three different occasions], "discernable" for "discernible"; "discrete" for "discreet") that someone with a stronger background in the increasingly scarce job of copyediting might have caught.

Baird has also published a booklet of tales by David Barker. Regrettably, these four stories do not represent Barker at his best. The title story is in the subgenre of "corporate horror"— a subgenre pioneered by Thomas Ligotti's pungent short novel *My Work Is Not Yet Done* (2002) and some of the tales of Mark Samuels. But Barker's tale is far longer than it needs to be, and its relatively bland and flat narrative tone fails to engender dramatic tensity, although the plot—which involves an office worker who sees the ghosts of some of his former colleagues re-enact a murder that occurred forty years earlier—has the potential to be an effective weird tale. Another office story, "Nearly But Quite Separate," is somewhat better, but still lacks focus and direction. But "The Flower Girl" is well worth reading, telling hypnotically of a decadent painter who lives in a house on a high mountaintop and paints women who have been crushed to death when their nearby houses fell over the edge of a cliff.

I applaud Baird's mere decision to publish this booklet and hope that others may follow his example. I estimate that this publication contains about 25,000 words of fiction—a convenient size if one is introducing the work of some promising novice or even of an established veteran like Barker.

Graeme Phillips has been editing *Cyäegha* from his eyrie in Scotland since 2008. It generally appears twice a year, although there was only one issue in 2018. It is more along the lines of the historical "fanzine" than *The Audient Void*, as it is clearly focused on Lovecraft (the title, I take it, is a playful adaptation of the name of Lovecraft's most celebrated creation), with both the virtues and drawbacks that such a focus entails.

The bulk of the three issues under review is devoted to fiction. Of the four lengthy stories in issue 20, the first—"Dancing for Azathoth" by Jaap Boekenstein and Tais Teng—exhibits some of the more regrettable features of "fan" fiction, merely playing with elements from Lovecraft's Dreamlands (with nods to Clark Ashton Smith's Zothique and Robert W. Chambers) but scarcely amounting to a serious work of fiction in its own right. But the other two stories are of a very different order. Mark J. Appleton's "The Poison Gate" is a sophisticated hybrid of Lovecraftian and science fictional elements, dealing with a kind of super-bionic woman (centuries old, it appears) in the far future exploring an ancient library on the planet Celaeno 25. At times the scientific terminology overwhelms the reader, but the story is nonetheless written with great power. Robert M. Price, a prolific and unrepentant pasticheur who at times has trouble taking Lovecraft (and himself) seriously, has written an effective tale ("Invaders from the Black Lagoon") that melds "The Shadow over Innsmouth" with the film *The Creature from the Black Lagoon*. Boekenstein contributes an able story on his own, "Creator of Life and Death," about a woman who seeks her lover and protector, André—and comes to believe that she herself may be a kind of Frankenstein's monster assembled from the disparate parts of women André had loved. The story is not Lovecraftian, but it is grimly powerful.

This story, it turns out, was translated by Phillips from Dutch. Indeed, the two subsequent issues of *Cyäegha* (the first coedited by Mike Jensen, the second by Jaap Boekestein and Marcel Orie) present an array of fiction and other work written by Dutch authors, some of it taken from the anthology *Lovecraft in de polder,* edited by Laura Scheepers (EdgeZero, 2018). The stories are quite a mixed bag, but their mere presentation here is illuminating in allowing Anglophone readers to grasp how Lovecraft's influence is manifested in non-English-speaking countries.

Dutch interest in Lovecraft began no later than the 1960s, when the first Dutch translations of his work were published. In the 1970s Eddy C. Bertin (1944–2018) emerged as a leading figure, both as a critic and as a fiction writer; issue 22 contains interesting brief assessments of his career by Jan J. B. Kuipers and Paul van Leeuwenkamp. Of the stories contained in issues 21 and 22, some of the better ones are "Of the Sea," by Abram Hertroys, a short mood piece about a "nymph" who emerges out of the sea and has curious revelations for the man who finds her; "Games Night," by Johan Klein Hanevald, an effective attempt to base a story on a character who has played the *Call of Cthulhu* role-playing game; "The Yellow Smear," also by Hanevald, a moderately engaging story about a married couple who suddenly find a painting by Richard Upton Pickman in their house; and Marcel Orie's "The Feast under the Catacombs," a kaleidoscopic, impressionistic tale about dead pirates (some of them being figures in Lovecraft's story "The Terrible Old Man") who have a kind of life in the town of Wurmwater.

There is also an array of fine poetry in the three issues, although *Cyäegha* largely prints poetry as fillers (just as *Weird Tales* tended to do). But the work of DJ Tyer, Frank Coffman (who has written a lively retelling of "Pickman's Model"), Cardinal Cox, and others is not to be missed.

With these two journals, along with Robert M. Price's revived *Crypt of Cthulhu* and several others one could mention, it can safely be said that the fanzine is alive and well. While modern technology has allowed these publications to be more impressive in appearance than their predecessors, the issue of overall quality remains a persistent problem; but then, it is a problem that besets professional publishing as well. In continuing a century-old tradition, these fanzines allow contemporary readers to gain a glimpse of how this untidy and obscure field evolved long before it was a bestselling phenomenon. That their editors and writers are working largely out of love and devotion to the field is a methodology we might all benefit from practicing.

Ramsey's Rant: Just a Coincidence

Ramsey Campbell

One of the writer's best friends—this writer's, at any rate—is coincidence. I don't mean as an element in fiction. For decades I've regretted the contrivance that begins my first published novel. Perhaps credulity isn't strained too much by having the fellow who causes a fatal car accident prove to be anthropophagous, but what possessed me to have the accident chop off the driver's arm as an attractive titbit for the cannibal? Sadly, so much of the book depends on this device that I saw no way of changing it, though I did rewrite the finale to accord the cannibal a more dramatic fate than simply toppling off a bike. I also came to deplore the scene in *The Nameless* where a member of the hotel staff conveniently leaves an occult magazine lying around in the lobby, and rewrote that scene too, relocating the magazine to a newsstand. Otherwise I try to leave my published stuff unaltered, however great the temptation to improve it. Once I started I might never stop.

Productive coincidences are another matter. I'm unsure to what extent my mind is alert, however unconsciously, for incidents I can incorporate in the work in progress, but it's certainly the case that opportune events and details frequently present themselves for use. Alas, I've subsumed most of them so successfully that I can't identify them any more. One representative instance: while I was writing *The Grin of the Dark,* a novel to which silent comedian Tubby Thackeray is central, Jenny and I watched a set of the early Astaire-Rogers musicals, and I was disconcerted to realise that the men's club in *Top Hat,* where Astaire disturbs the silence, is called the Thackeray Club. But our life—Jenny's and mine—seems so full of concurrences that we might imagine we attract them, like the protagonist of Stephen Barr's witty tale "I Am a Nucleus" (*Galaxy Science Fiction,* February 1957). What do our experiences mean, if anything? Let me cite some on the way to seeking a conclusion.

It's only mildly astonishing that a prolific contributor to *Weird Tales*—G. G. Pendarves—made her final home less than a mile from mine, which helps to explain why her grave is as close as that too, in Rake Lane Cemetery (to be precise, plot number 73 in section 14C, where her coffin is apparently the topmost in the family grave). Her real name was Gladys Gordon Trenery, but I shouldn't make too much of the fact that a Gladys Trenery lived next door to my childhood home. And it's hardly surprising that Pendarves used nearby Parkgate as the setting of a story—"Thing of Darkness"—as I did in "The Ferries," though she disguises it as Seagate. Again, is it more than a minor coincidence that when I wrote Edward Anthony a letter care of our publishers in appreciation of his book *Thy Rod and Staff,* he proved to have lived as a child in this very road? But other incidents are more elaborate—veritable efflorescences of coincidence.

Bear with me while I expound. Many years ago I was among the judges of the Constable Award, a literary prize, where each of us read half a dozen anonymised novels and recommended two of them for our fellow panellists to read. Soon a judge sent around a campus novel, narrated alternately by two lecturers, a former African National Congress activist and an ex-nun. I'd read just the first two chapters when I knew that the authors were friends of ours, who still live just half a mile from us. For the next round of elimination the judges met, and I would have had to declare my connection if Maggie Gee hadn't objected to the book. She famously persuaded her fellow Booker Prize judges to remove Martin Amis's *London Fields* from the shortlist (a capitulation David Lodge says he regrets), and in the case of the collaboration submitted to Constable she complained that a scene in which the ex-nun is embarrassed by her nunnish underwear while changing in a London boutique was plainly a male fetishist's fantasy. Once the novel fell at a hurdle I was able to reveal that the chapter was written by none other than a former nun.

Years later I wrote the introduction to Niki Flynn's memoir *Dances with Werewolves*. Let me assure you I'm still talking about the same conglomeration of coincidence. In the introduction I cited Maggie Gee's reading of the collaborative novel as evidence that we can't control or indeed predict how audiences receive our work. When Niki launched the book in London, Jenny and I travelled to support her. With hours to spare we visited the Tate Modern gallery, which had mounted a surrealist exhibition. As we entered the first room we came face to face with our friend the ex-nun. To summarise, more than two hundred miles away from home and by pure coincidence we met someone who lives half a mile from us and who was cited in my introduction to the book that was the reason we were in London.

The house that faces ours seems to have been drawn into the network—certainly its present occupiers, Melanie and Nick. Melanie is a cellist and music teacher who turned out to give classes at St Edward's, my old grammar school, ten miles away across the river. In itself that may be minor, but add this. Her mother Sylvia (gone from us, alas) once told me that her nephew wrote science fiction. Ah, I said warily, bracing myself to be asked to read his unpublished trilogy and see it into print: what's his name? Charles Platt was the answer, not just an accomplished author who edited *New Worlds* after Mike Moorcock stood down but my genial host on one of my earliest teenage jaunts to London. Sylvia Jean Caveley did indeed become his aunt by her second marriage. And let me mention one more congruence. We introduced Melanie and Nick to a favourite Nepalese restaurant, Da Gurkha, ten miles away across the river (in quite a different direction than my old school). During dinner I glanced across the floor to see, among the party at the table opposite, the lady from whom they'd bought their house in our road. She lives on our side of the river, further from the restaurant than we do, and had never previously visited it—indeed, was there purely at the suggestion of the organiser of the meal.

What do I take from all this? Simply a sense that reality has an intermittent tendency to form patterns, of which we folk are one more element. It's a theme upon which I touched in a story called "The Pattern", written more than forty years ago, long before any of these events. I would also say that a happy coincidence started my career. When I submitted my first Lovecraftian tales to August Derleth, purely for his opinion and with no thought they would be published, I had no idea that (as I learned later from our correspondence) he felt he'd exhausted his own ability to produce such fiction. Since his Mythos stories were designed to keep Lovecraft's name alive by association, he may well have seen my own efforts as a welcome substitute, however much editorial work they required. Horrid cliché it may be, but I really think I arrived in the right place at the right time with the right material.

I'm haunted by one more coincidence, if that's what it is. For more years than I can remember I've found myself glancing at clocks to see that they're showing 7.47, so often that the digits have acquired an ominous significance. Could they refer to an aeroplane, or a time of the morning, or both? Perhaps both will coincide one day, and I'll know their significance at last. Let's hope they prove to be worth waiting for.

The Dark Gnosis of D. L. Myers

Leigh Blackmore

D. L. MYERS. *Oracles from the Black Pool.* Introduction by K. A. Opperman. Cover, design, and interior illustrations by Dan Sauer. New York: Hippocampus Press, 2019. 136 pp. $15.00 tpb. ISBN: 978-1-61498-243-2.

D. L. Myers—who he? Well, readers ought not to confuse the author of the weird verse collection *Oracles from the Black Pool* with another D. L. Myers (female), who published a poetry collection called *Leaving Logic Lane*, and an ebook of fantasy fiction called *The Golden Light Trilogy.*

The D. L. Myers with whom we are concerned is a mysterious poetic personage (K. A. Opperman's introduction acknowledges that Myers is somewhat reclusive) who writes verse rather in the vein of H. P. Lovecraft, Clark Ashton Smith, and Robert E. Howard. He lives in the mist-shrouded Skagit Valley in the state of Washington. His previous poetic work has appeared in venues including *Spectral Realms, Halloween Howlings, The Audient Void,* and K. A. Opperman's collection *The Crimson Tome*. According to a note on him at the H. P. Lovecraft Film Festival site, he is also an accomplished reader of poetry, and he does a weekly video poetry reading of contemporary and classic weird poets, as well as his own work, which he posts on his blog www.vulravin.blogspot.com. Other readings can be found at YouTube.

Oracles from the Black Pool is another substantial collection of weird verse from Hippocampus Press which adds to that publisher's illustrious roster of modern weird collections by such poets as Wade German, Ashley Dioses, K. A. Opperman, Adam Bolivar, Michael Fantina, Fred Phillips, Park Barnitz, George Sterling, Nora May French, Donald Sidney-Fryer, and Leah Bodine Drake. The volume is worthy of representation amidst this company, for though it appears Myers has been publishing his work for less than a decade, it is work of high quality and imaginative force.

The volume is divided into seven sequences plus a section of tributes. The sections are 1) Yorehaven (named after a town invented by Opperman but extensively used by Myers), 2) Acolytes (seasonal poems), (3) The Summons (nature poems), (4) The Star's Prisoner (cosmic poems), 5) The Canker Within (poems of horror), 6) Temple River Goddess (femmes fatales), and 7) O Dark Muse (poems of Sorcery and Creativity)

While the subject matter of a few of the verses is hoary and well-worn (werewolf, vampire), the bulk of the collection is refreshingly free of over-utilized themes; and even where Myers occasionally treads familiar ground, the vitality of his expression, whether in rhyme or in free verse, overcomes what might have been a limitation in lesser hands. Myers uses an entertaining variety of meter and form—the latter ranging from long and short (some as brief as a single quatrain) poems, through sonnets and ballads, to haiku and prose poems. His work is largely non-programmatic—that is, there may not be a "story" to each piece, yet the overwhelming sense of weird and oft-ultraterrene atmosphere created by the poet can only be redolent of such masters and Lovecraft and Smith. (I will not quibble about the very occasional inconsistency of scansion in a m few poems.) Themes of paganism, and of dark roads, streets, and forests; of cold and ice; of dead or dying stars; of night animals from owls to Death's-head moths and ravens; of Death personified; and an omnipresent sense of loss, fate, and doom combine to make this collection one for the aficionado to savor. We even find here a poem about the Victorian serial killer Jack the Ripper.

Several poems in Section 7 are dedicated to K. A. Opperman. The poetic tributes to Myers in Section 8 are by Opperman, Ashley Dioses, and Adam Bolivar—the three other poets who make up a self-nominated coterie of weird poets they have dubbed "The Crimson Circle."

Mention must be made of the superb photocollage illustrations by Dan Sauer that decorate the volume. Not only do these amplify the atmosphere of the poems to fine advantage, but they prove Sauer fit to stand shoulder-to-shoulder with weird photocollage artists such as Harry O. Morris and J. K. Potter.

Oracles from the Dark Pool offers a unique, dark gnosis of poetic insights into the darker side of humanity and of the natural and unnatural worlds. An essential purchase for the devotee.

More "Thing"

Darrell Schweitzer

JOHN W. CAMPBELL, JR. *Frozen Hell*. Edited by John Gregory Betancourt. Rockville MD: Wildside Press, 2019. 158 pp. $29.95 hc. ISBN: 978-1-4794-4283-6; $15.00 tpb. ISBN: 978-1-4794-4282-9.

John W. Campbell's novella "Who Goes There?" has been more or less continuously in print since 1938. It has been filmed twice: first in 1951 as *The Thing from Another World;* then there is John Carpenter's iconic *The Thing* (1982); three times if you want to count the prequel, also confusingly entitled *The Thing* (2017), and is widely recognized as one of the greatest science fiction horror stories of all time. It is probably a little late to ask if it's any good. That would be rather like asking if "The Call of Cthulhu" is any good, or important. Yes, the verdict seems to be in.

The discovery of an earlier, longer version entitled *Frozen Hell* is an event of more than just academic interest, but it is not going to supplant the classic we all know. Alec Nevala-Lee explains in a preface that the work was found among Campbell's papers at Harvard, consisting of 20 pages in fair copy, probably typed by Campbell's first wife Dona, plus 112 pages of a complete rough draft. The two have been spliced together, not quite smoothly, as occasional repetitions of lines or descriptions show.

Robert Silverberg, in a more detailed introduction, gives us the complete back story. This version was written first and intended for *Argosy* magazine. By the mid-'30s, John Campbell's career was in a precarious position. His super-science epics were going out of fashion at *Astounding*. He could not live on his moody Don A. Stuart stories, though they were still welcome. *Amazing Stories* had one of his novels in inventory already and paid low and slow. *Wonder Stories* had just morphed into *Thrilling Wonder Stories,* for which Campbell agreed to write a series of formulaic imitations of the late Stanley G. Weinbaum, the Penton and Blake series, one of which, "The Brain-Stealers of Mars," treats the shape-changing premise of the later "Who Goes There?" as comedy. Fortunately, Jack Byrne at *Argosy* was increasingly interested in science fiction and recruiting science fiction writers. *Argosy* around this time published Donald Wandrei and Jack Williamson, plus "fantastics" by such regulars as Edgar Rice Burroughs and "George Challis" (a.k.a. Frederick Faust, better known as Max Brand), and, slightly later, Eando Binder's *Lords of Creation* (1939). In a moment of what can only have been desperation, the magazine ran E. Hoffmann Price and Otis Adelbert Kline's ghodawful serial "Satans on Saturn" in 1940 but redeemed itself with Henry Kuttner and C. L. Moore's "Earth's Last Citadel" in 1943. *Argosy* also began to feature a lot of slick fantasy, usually by Robert Arthur, which anticipated much of what Campbell would publish in *Unknown*.

So by 1936 or 1937 the time was ripe for Campbell to try to expand his markets and try for *Argosy*. He met with Byrne, proposed the story, and wrote it. What we have here, plus or minus a few sentences Campbell might have revised, is that version. It is eight chapters long. In the last five chapters it becomes more or less the same story we know as "Who Goes There?"

Byrne rejected it. He put his finger very precisely on what was wrong with it: ". . . it's a good idea, good yarn, good writing. There aren't any characters in it. It's got a bunch of minor characters, but no major characters." Campbell actually quoted that in a letter to a friend and agreed with it, but, frankly, even in the final, classic version, he never quite conquered the problem. Most of the characters in "Who Goes There?" are still just names, some with character tags to help you tell them apart. I will confess that when I went to write a story for John Betancourt's Wildside Press "tribute" anthology, *Short Things: Tales Inspired by "Who Goes There?"* (2019), and had to focus on the characters (since my story was intended to be very intense and paranoiac), I had to make of a cheat sheet of who all the characters were and keep it in hand while rereading Campbell. One character proved to be a typo.

A simple way to describe those first three chapters of *Frozen Hell*, published here for the first time, and to explain their relationship to the classic version, goes like this: Imagine if three new acts to Shakespeare's *Hamlet* were discovered, making the five-act play into an eight-act play. They all take place before the action of the play we know, showing Hamlet at college in Wittenberg, how he gets along with Rosencrantz and Guildenstern, his reaction to the news that his father is dead, his journey back to Elsinore, his rising suspicions of foul play, etc. This material might be of interest to readers now, but in 1600 or thereabouts it would have detracted from the tension of the play. Shakespeare would have known to cut it out. When Campbell revised *Frozen Hell* into "Who Goes There?" he did the same. The first three chapters relate the discovery of the alien spacecraft under the ice, its accidental destruction, how the frozen alien was hauled back to camp, etc. In the final version this is told far more effectively in a vivid flashback of about a page, not in three chapters.

Campbell later wrote to an apprentice writer named Isaac Asimov, "When you have trouble with the beginning of a story, that is because you are starting in the wrong place, and almost certainly too soon."

Lesson learned. It is not recorded if Campbell ever submitted the short version, "Who Goes There?," to Jack Byrne, but he did submit it to F. Orlin Tremaine at *Astounding*. While the story was under consideration, Tremaine was promoted to be in charge of all the Street & Smith pulps, which meant there was no editor of *Astounding* and he asked Campbell to succeed him. In the first year or so, Campbell was in effect a first reader, and Tremaine approved everything Campbell wanted to buy, so actually Tremaine bought "Who Goes There?" even though it was published in a Campbell issue under the Don A. Stuart byline. *Frozen Hell,* the long version, was permanently shelved. Republished now, it is of interest for showing us how Campbell, after false starts, arrived at his famous classic. Would-be writers should compare to two, to learn about pacing and structure. By taking out the "adventure story" elements in those first few chapters, plus some clumsy exposition (e.g., a character's dream used to explain what a shape-changing creature might be able to do), Campbell had a tightly focused science fiction horror story, in the claustrophobic setting of an Antarctic base. This is the story that today (even if you need a cheat sheet in hand) is still powerful and effective. The Thing remains one of the all-time great literary monsters, right up there with Cthulhu and Count Dracula. Nothing can take that away.

The present volume has a striking cover and excellent interior illustrations by Bob Eggleton, and also includes opening chapters of a sequel that editor John Betancourt proposes to write. It is a competent job. It may turn out to be very good. The U.S. military discovers another spaceship and another Thing in the Antarctic. Very hush-hush. Having read the 1938 "report," they don't intend to allow any slip-ups. But a frozen Thing seems to have telepathically persuaded a guard to turn a heater in its direction. Drip, drip . . .

Polluting Gods: Liminality, Devolution, and the Defamiliarization of Human Identity in Blackwood's "The Wendigo" and Kipling's "The Mark of the Beast"

Michael J. Abolafia

The intellectual imaginary of the late nineteenth-century Gothic is preoccupied, to an almost pathological degree, with the biopolitics and aesthetics of disintegration, disfiguration, and devolution—horrifying transmogrifications occurring among bodies, spaces, and even "metropoles," or whole civilizations. These "categorical breakdowns" illuminate a constellation of interrelated anxieties that all find their centers of gravity in the concept of the liminal. Although the literature of the supernatural has, since its earliest inception, deployed "in-betweenness" and transitionality to signify uncertainty and uncomfortable borderlands,[1] the late nineteenth century bore witness to the emergence of crucial epistemological disjunctions that reshaped the ways in which human beings viewed biological, spiritual, and psychological reality.

These transubstantiations—occurring crucially in the realms of the biological sciences, with the advent of Darwin and Linnaean taxonomy, and in psychology, with the paradigm-shift wrought by Freud's estranging of the knowable self from the unconscious matter that imperceptibly shapes the human—produced tremendous anxiety, such that, as Kelly Hurley writes, "the idea of a stable human identity [was de-

---

This essay was composed for Professor Roger Luckhurst's spring 2016 course on Gothic Literature at Columbia University. Thanks to Professor Luckhurst for his feedback and intellectual generosity.

1. Borderlands separating the known from the unknown, life from death, the human from the abhuman or the bestial, among others.

molished] . . . giving imaginative warrant to the richly loathsome variety of abhuman abominations that the Gothic went on to produce" (205). The fin-de-siècle Gothic—a literature, fittingly, written at the interstices of two centuries—reconfigures and recontextualizes the "liminal" anxieties that had been characteristic of Gothic fiction since its uncanny inception in the febrile nightmares of Horace Walpole and Ann Radcliffe. The crossing of thresholds, often embodying the unspeakable terrors of socio-sexual transgressions of inheritance and patrilineality, or the metaphysically uncrossable borderlands separating the material body from the eternal soul, became displaced, in the Victorian worldview, by a mounting disquietude toward these "new" models of the human.

In Hurley's words, "the proliferation of Gothic representations of abhumanness at the fin de siècle may be partly attributed to the destabilizing effects of nineteenth-century Darwinian science," which, in its re-categorization of human beings as having an intrinsic, intimate connection with the "animals" from which they evolved, dissolved the animal-human binary, and presented all species—human beings included—as ultimately "impermanent, metamorphic, and liable to extinction" (195), rather than as the fixed, immutable masters at the summit of the Judeo-Christian Great Chain of Being. The accelerated taxonomic activity of the Victorian era positioned the human and the animal on a continuum, instantiating the profoundly disconcerting sense that natural order is *dis*order, and that human selves and human bodies are characterized by admixture, fluxity, and in-betweenness: they are "always-already in a state of indifferentiation, or undergoing metamorphoses into a bizarre assortment of human/not-human configurations" (Hurley, *Gothic Body* 10). The Victorian conceptualization of the human often marries marginality, or liminality, and abhumanity. Whereas in the fictions of the First Wave of the Gothic, devolution, disintegration, and abhumanness are related to "transgressive" social phenomena—to homosexuality, madness, criminality, or female eroticism, for example—many of the defining texts of the Victorian Gothic present the susceptibility of *all human* subjects to the perils of bodily and psychological abhumanness. The Gothic fictions of Rudyard Kipling and Algernon Blackwood evince a thematic interest in Darwinian evolution and the Freudian reimagining of human subjectivity as fractured, unstable and chthonically indeterminate.

In this way, Victorian narratives of the Gothic, like Rudyard Kipling's colonially marginal "The Mark of the Beast" (1890) and Algernon Blackwood's metaphysical "The Wendigo" (1910)[2] deploy liminal spatialities, temporalities, and monstrously in-between transfigurations to suggest that the imperiled subjectivity, defamiliarized, dehumanized, and biologically devolved, is always hovering on the unstable precipice of self-dissolution. The hybrid, amalgamated horrors in these stories, uncomfortably straddling the borderland between human and ab-/non-human, conceptualize Gothic liminality as an engine of anthropocentric destabilization, such that both self and body become dismembered, disjointed, and thereby "polluted." And, crucially, these contagions, because of their liminality, threaten not only individual subjectivity, but collective and national identity as well.

Rudyard Kipling's "Mark of the Beast" narrativizes the dangers of liminality and expresses the colonial anxiety toward the Other and the decidedly Victorian revulsion towards the disintegration of the human body and the human subjectivity. The story begins with an almost casual declaration of the disconcerting marginality of the colonial hinterland:

> East of Suez, some hold, the direct control of Providence ceases; Man being there handed over to the power of Gods and Devils of Asia, and the Church of England Providence only exercising an occasional and modified supervision in the case of Englishmen. (208)

Here, Kipling asserts outright that the "unnecessary horrors" (208) that his protagonists will encounter are intrinsically linked to the colonial zone, sequestered from Providence and the "civilizing," organizational institution of the Church of England. The text also instantiates a liminal temporality in sit-

---

2. In this essay, the texts of both stories will be cited from Darryl Jones's *Horror Stories* (2014).

uating the narrative on New Year's Day, an uncanny threshold between the death of the previous year and the birth of the new one. At the "ends of the empire" (208) the colonists gather, the allegorized forces of "civilization" massed together in their "secure" compound in "the hills" (208). Kipling counterposes the homosocial gaiety and revelry of the Englishmen—"there was a general closing up of ranks . . . I remember that we sang 'Auld Lang Syne' with our feet in the Polo Championship Cup . . . and swore that we were all dear friends" (209)—with the uncontrollable diabolism and violence of the outside, of which the officers—some of whom "had not seen twenty white faces for a year" (208)—are singularly aware.

They spend time "taking stock of our losses in dead and disabled" (209) and, when the hapless Fleete becomes too drunk to stand, they "formed a Guard of Dishonour" to take him home—a language suggesting the extent to which the men conceive of themselves as a martial unit. As Rod Edmond writes, "a complex . . . relationship binds the narrator of Kipling's story to Strickland and Fleete," a relationship that is "based on the codes and practices of the public school, the army and the colonial service, and reinforced by the isolation and incipient paranoia of living as a dominant but minority group" (141). Fleete's inebriated transgression, wherein he "grinds the ashes of his cigar-butt on the forehead of the red, stone image of Hanuman" (209)—a monkey deity, a "gray ape of the hills" (209) that evokes the Darwinian devolution at the heart of the text's production of horror—triggers the appearance of the liminal "Silver Man" who will come to haunt Fleete and his imperialist compatriots. The Silver Man "came out of a recess behind the image of the god," and "had no face because he was a leper . . . and his disease was upon him" (210). The story's depiction of the Silver Man—an appellation that refuses his humanity by associating him with a precious colonial commodity—is always expressed in less-than-human terms: the people who fill the temple "seemed to spring from the earth," and the Silver Man is presented as being bestially incapable of speech, "mewling like an otter" instead (210).

The Silver Man's leprosy situates him as a liminal entity,

uncategorizably poised between life and death, alive but putrefying and decomposing. For Rod Edmond, "Leprosy . . . is a boundary disease par excellence" that, in the English colonial imaginary, served to "re-establish the categories and boundaries that define our relation to the world by keeping the clean from the unclean, and thereby rescuing purity from danger . . . the leper inhabited a no-man's land, a limit zone" (11–13). The figure's marginality threatens the colonial enterprise: he infects Fleete, such that his mastery over nature falters. Upon his returning home, Fleete's "five horses" and terriers "seemed to have gone mad" (212) and flee the compound, while the markers of Fleete's humanity—speech, manners, and sleeping habits—become increasingly estranged and animalistic under the aegis of the retributive Mark of the Beast. The narrator explicitly contrasts Fleete's eating his raw meat "like a beast" with the "society as refined and elevating as ours" (212), and he observes that "there was something excessively out of order" (214) about Fleete's uncanny manner.

When the narrator and Strickland hear the distant baying of a wolf, they recognize that "The human spirit must have been giving way all day and have died out with the twilight" (215)—with twilight signifying a liminal transition between human and abhuman. Dumoise, a medical man of an obviously materialist inclination, tries in vain to classify Fleete's bodily disintegration as a kind of "hydrophobia" or mania, but, as the narrator remarks, "The affair was beyond any human and rational experience" (215). The leper, they realize, has brought Fleete to "degradation," and "His flesh was not the flesh of a clean man" (217)—they continually refer to the officer as "it" rather than "he." Their torturing the leper—occurring, again, at dawn—results in the restoration of Fleete's humanity, but at the cost of theirs. This victory is a Pyrrhic one, simultaneously exposing their *collective* weakness as Westerners: they "had disgraced ourselves as Englishmen for ever" (219). The horror of the liminal lies precisely in its dissolution and destabilization of boundaries. Polysemously perverse and anxiously uncontainable, the liminal denies easy categorization.

Mary Douglas's *Purity and Danger* conceptualizes the body as a "model which can stand for any bounded system. Its boundaries can represent any boundaries which are threatened or precarious . . . Any structure of ideas is vulnerable at its margins . . . The anxiety about bodily margins expresses danger to group survival" (116). Fleete's devolution into a bestial "it," faceless and devoid of self like the liminal Silver Man, embodies these communitarian anxieties: Strickland and the narrator are forced to confront, at story's end, the destabilizing idea that the "small progress"—Strickland's modus operandi, it is said, is to "overmatch" the natives "with their own weapons" (210)—of the colonial endeavor is ultimately unstable, untenable, destined to collapse at the margins.

Fleete is overtaken and transformed by a figure at the interstices into a liminoid monstrosity, and eventually returned to "normalcy"—but only through the Westerners' rejection of their own systems of medical knowledge and proper conduct: the torture of the Silver Man, an act too bestial "to be printed" (218) and thus deferred by a textual gap, suggests the failure of the "civilizing" enterprise altogether. The Englishmen, in this sense, are infected by the Silver Man's devolved liminality and transformed into figures of the barbarous atavism that they themselves fear among the "natives." The liminal, in Kipling's text, is closely aligned with colonial anxieties towards "going native"—a dissolution of the categorical distinctions between colonizer and colonized, pure and infected, "civilized" and "savage," "progress" and devolution or regression. All human beings are, in the liminal space, vulnerable to being "infected" by the liminoid—becoming, in effect, themselves liminal, beyond the "rational," compartmentalized categories of human knowledge and human biological reality. The liminal, precisely because of its fluctuating and uncategorizable nature and its fluid capacity to move among and across borders, stages the monstrous hybridism in Kipling's story as a *communal* and *collective* and *national*, rather than merely individual, locus of contagion.

Max Nordau's widely influential *Degeneration* (1892–93) is perhaps the defining ur-text for fin-de-siècle theorizations of societal decay. For Nordau, the "hysteria and degeneration" characteristic of his waning epoch had "always existed," but only recently, because of the "multitudes of discoveries and innovations" that "burst abruptly" onto the scene, posed a "danger to civilization" and to the "life of the whole community" (597). Nordau aestheticizes decay in terms of bacteriological pathology: shortly after these declarations, he calls social transgressions "maladies" and models his own conception of moral depredation on parasites, *bacillus,* vermin. Nordau the apocalyptic diagnostician was countered by a whole host of "progress"-minded imperialists, such as the minor philosopher Alfred Egmont Hake, who proposed an antidote to fin-de-siècle malaise: "to be practical, energetic, daring pioneers heading the march of progress" (quoted in Edmond 12). In this way, Victorian discourses of national, communal progress are dialectically opposed to the logic of devolution, regression, and psychopathological sickness that coalesce around Nordau's fallen West—a dialectic of progress/health and devolution/sickness that Kipling exploits through his liminal destabilizations.

Although written twenty years after Kipling's Gothic tale, and situated in a decidedly different post-colonial context, a similar fin-de-siècle logic of liminal destabilization animates Algernon Blackwood's "The Wendigo." Set in the liminal hinterlands of the vast, untameable Canadian wilds, Blackwood's story is centered on a hunting party comprised of five individuals: the doctor Cathcart, his seminary school nephew Simpson, their backwoods guides, Joseph Défago and Hank Davis, and the cook, Punk. From the story's inception, Défago is marked as a marginal figure:

> Joseph Défago was a French 'Canuck,' who had strayed from his native Province of Quebec . . . when the Canadian Pacific Railway was a-building . . . He was deeply susceptible, moreover, to that singular spell which the wilderness lays upon certain lonely natures. (378)

Described as "imaginative and melancholy" (379), Défago occupies a racially interstitial space: he is both a native Canuck and a Frenchman, and he is emphatically marked as an Other, given to fits of "moroseness" foisted upon him by "civilization." Revealingly, the five characters' relationship is one of camaraderie and even mutual deference: they sing "old *voyageur* songs" (378), and the comparatively uncouth Hank "agreed to dam" his "river of expletives" out of "respect for his old hunting boss, Dr Cathcart" (379). Moreover, the story suggests that in the wild, men "lose superficial . . . distinctions," becoming instead "human beings working together for a common end" (384). Like the English occupiers of India in Kipling's club tale, they form a kind of homosocial unit—a "garrison," in Margaret Atwood's conception—against the unyielding and impenetrable outside: a "listening forest" that "stole forward and enveloped them" (380) in the "jaws of the wilderness" (383). These personifications of the natural world operate in much the same way that Défago is "subtly in league with the soul of the woods" (383): they imply a dissolution of the boundaries separating the human and the beyond, giving the wilderness an agency that human beings lack in comparison.

Défago—whose name faintly echoes, etymologically, the Latin *-phage,* referring to consumption and cannibalism and often associated with contagion—is capable of "merging his figure into the surrounding blackness in a way that only wild men and animals understand . . . the forest absorbed him into herself" (383–85), and his liminoid status, mediating between cultures and the "civilized" and "uncivilized" binary, is precisely what makes him prey to the disassembling horror of the Wendigo. Crucially, Simpson positions Défago as all that "stood between him and a pitiless death by exhaustion and starvation" (385): an assertion of dependency and Défago's status as a figure whose dissolution threatens group survival. Upon crossing the Hudson Bay—a literal movement across thresholds—they reach Fifty Island Water, which is explicitly cartographed as a fantastical, marginal zone: there are hints of "woodland gods" and the islands "floated like the fairy barques of some enchanted fleet" (387). The locus of anxiety is related in terms of the locale's inability to be taxonomized, since it "would never be known or trodden" (392). The cumulative effect of the liminal setting into which Défago and Simpson are cast—they are "alone together" (398)—is one of dislocation and disintegration, hovering at the precipice of being consumed by the "living forest."

Défago's marginal subjectivity occupies an uneasy racial interstice between the "civilized" West and the "uncivilized," abominable Other, reflecting the fin-de-siècle anxiety toward the dissolution of markers and boundaries of racial identity. As Jack Halberstam explains, referring to the Victorian "category crisis" of identity, monsters "always represents the disruption of categories, the destruction of boundaries, and the presence of impurities . . . The Gothic monster, moreover, as a creature of mixed blood, breaks down the very categories that constitute . . . racial difference" (76). And, indeed, it is Défago's "Latin" blood that differentiates him from the other members of the cohort (aside, perhaps, from the "real African," Punk), placing him at a marginal borderland which renders him uniquely vulnerable to possession by the Wendigo, an interstitial creature that seems to be constituted of wild nature itself, with its "windy, crying" voice, its smelling like a "lion," and its preternatural control over the wastes. The text's first presentation of the numinous encounter with the Wendigo, when Simpson hears Défago weeping in the tent and witnesses him being dragged from the inside of the tent (connoting safety) and across the threshold to the terrifying, shadowy outside, immediately activates a sense of monstrous, category-crossing hybridity: first, Défago's cries are an "intimate, human sound," but by sentence's end, they become "so incongruous, so pitifully incongruous" (394). Incongruity, here, implies a denial of categories; it's linked to the monstrous, the imbalanced, and the ill-proportioned. The hunters' transgression into the interstitial space of the wilderness—its vastness uncategorized and uncategorizable—allows for the borderlands between the known and the unknown, the human and abhuman, to be altogether collapsed.

"The pale gleam of the dawn" (395), another liminal temporality, heralds the beginning of the garrison's real horrors. When Défago abruptly exits the campsite, hysterical and maniacal, Simpson follows his footsteps and finds this:

> In the last hundred yards or so, he saw that they had grown gradually into the semblance of the parent tread . . . Smaller, neater, more cleanly modeled, they formed now an exact and careful duplicate of the larger tracks beside them. The feet that produced them had, therefore, also changed. (402)

Défago is *transformed* into the monstrous, the "abominable" (401) Wendigo, his feet—an anatomical and bodily marker separating human from non-human, especially in a hunting context—rendered "an exact and careful duplicate" of the creature's. This ignites within Simpson a maelstrom of panic: the categories between human and abhuman now wholly disintegrated, he repeatedly describes his "disorganized . . . mind and spirit" and his "disorganized sensations" that the "dislocating experience" of "wizardry and horror" (401–5) forced him to confront—terrors that "shatter" him (403). Blackwood's deployment of an idiom of dislocation, disintegration, and, most notably, disorganization all suggest the perils of the borderland. The liminal terror of the Wendigo, it should be said, operates along multivalent registers, suggesting

> Euro-Western consumption of indigenous peoples, lands and resources . . . Characters suffering possession by the Wındigo might represent either the colonizer or the colonized, as the roles of both imperialist conqueror and victim reflect states of excess and imbalance. (Weinstock 591)

Yet Blackwood, unlike Kipling, is less ambivalent in his assignation of wrongdoing, disgrace, and violence to the Western hunter-tourists. The colonialism-as-cannibalism trope is rejected by Blackwood at every turn. He marks Simpson as a "*canny* Scot" who has a "measure of balance" (401) and, despite the ills that befall his cohort, he repeatedly manages to "rebalance" himself: he "approached his normal equilibrium" (404) and "emerged victor in the end" (404)—far from the "imbalance" and "excess" implied by the Wendigo, liminally crossing thresholds between the supernatural and the natural. This contrasts starkly with the doom experienced by Défago, whose personality and individuality are completely obviated by the Wendigo's possession, and transformation, of his soul. At story's end, he walks "as of a thing moved by wires" (414)—he is puppet-like, uncannily inhuman—and his "face was more animal than human, the features drawn about into wrong proportions, the skin loose and hanging . . . a face so piteous, so terrible and so little like humanity" (416). He is *imbalanced*, disproportionate, disordered, dismembered. And, as the narrator relates, his "mind had fled beyond recall. And with it, too, had fled memory ... The 'something' that had constituted him 'individual' had vanished for ever" (420). His monstrous transfiguration destroys not only his corporeal physicality, but also the seat of his self: the mind, memory, the soul, that "something that had constituted him individual."

While Défago is dissolved—he dies at the story's close—the rest of the cohort remains largely unharmed, though the Wendigo "half-destroyed their reality" (415). In fact, they all "reduced" their "inner turmoil to a condition of more or less systematized order" (419). In Blackwood's narrative, conditions of liminality are, through Défago, directly linked to a reversal of human agency and order: the hunters become the hunted. Yet Blackwood, unlike Kipling, is motivated less by a desire to subtly expose the ills of imperialism than to leverage a critique of materialism. While the "materialist" Dr Cathcart finds that he has "insufficient knowledge" (407) to explain the events, it is Simpson, the "student of divinity," who "arranged his conclusions probably with the best, though not most scientific, appearance of order" (419)—who emerges as the least fragmented and most coherent self.

The fictions of both Algernon Blackwood and Rudyard Kipling, composed in a fin-de-siècle milieu, reflect the Victorian anxiety toward what Hurley identifies as the "exemplary abhuman body—liminal, admixed, nauseating, abominable" (509), a multivalent nexus of uncertainty, pollution, contagion, and self-dissolution. As interstitial creatures, the werewolf in Kipling's tale and the Wendigo in Blackwood's emblematize the boundless perils of the liminal: existing across ontological and biological taxonomies, they pose a threat to human epistemological structures of rational, organized knowledge. Liminalities, in Gothic fiction, represent uneasy sites of boundary-crossing, in which thresholds are collapsed and certainties destabilized. They provide, in effect, an interpretive lens through which the texts' core anxieties are made manifest. For Kipling, these fears cohere in a reversal of colonial power, the potentiality of indigenous retribution, and a fear of both individual and national regression—a failure of the "progress"-minded colonial enterprise. Blackwood's anxieties, on the other hand, evince a greater concern with racial hybridity, or liminality, and the susceptibility of the human to the metaphysical in liminal spaces. As Thomas L. Dumm notes,

> Etymologies suggest that *fear* once meant the experience of being between places of protection, in transit, in a situation analogous to the condition that is commonly referred to in contemporary ethnographic literature as liminality. (In Massumi 359)

That Gothic horror deploys the liminal in its production of fear, then, is far from surprising: perilous crossings, transgressions across boundaries, and uncertain thresholds resonate uniquely with age-old fears of devolution, disintegration, and defamiliarization—of place, space, time, and self.

Works Cited

Douglas, Mary. *Purity and Danger: An Analysis of Concepts of Pollution and Taboo*. New York: Praeger, 1966.

Edmond, Rod. *Leprosy and Empire: A Medical and Cultural History*. Cambridge: Cambridge University Press, 2006.

Halberstam, Judith. *Skin Shows: Gothic Horror and the Technology of Monsters*. Durham, NC: Duke University Press, 1995.

Hurley, Kelly. "British Gothic Fiction, 1885–1930." In Jerrold E. Hogle, ed. *The Cambridge Companion to the Modern Gothic*. Cambridge: Cambridge University Press, 2014. 180–225.

Hurley, Kelly. *The Gothic Body: Sexuality, Materialism, and Degeneration at the Fin de Siècle*. Cambridge: Cambridge University Press, 1996.

Jones, Darryl, ed. *Horror Stories: Classic Tales from Hoffmann to Hodgson*. New York: Oxford University Press, 2014.

Massumi, Brian. *The Politics of Everyday Fear*. Minneapolis: University of Minnesota Press, 1993.

Nordau, Max Simon. *Degeneration*. New York: Howard Fertig, 1968.

Weinstock, Jeffrey Andrew. *The Ashgate Encyclopedia of Literary and Cinematic Monsters*. Farnham, UK: Ashgate, 2014.

Unseen Worlds, Waiting to Be Discovered

Daniel Pietersen

MELISSA EDMUNDSON, ed. *Women's Weird: Strange Stories by Women 1890–1940*. Bath, UK: Handheld Press, 2019. 321 pp. $17.99 tpb. ISBN: 978-1-91276-624-6.

Think of weird fiction and, probably without even realising it, you will think of one thing: men. Whether it's H. P. Lovecraft's tentacled monstrosities, the decadent necromancies of Clark Ashton Smith, or Algernon Blackwood's eerie eco-horror, the canon of weird fiction, like many human endeavors, is dominated by male practitioners. Even now, when we have women such as Camilla Grudova, Nadia Bulkin, or Laura Mauro writing excellent weird fiction, the horror and related shelves of mainstream booksellers are still filled with multiple editions of works by the same dead white men. The implication is clear: women are newcomers to the genre, dabblers in a field already well-plowed.

Which makes Melissa Edmundson's anthology of early weird tales by women, from the first half of the twentieth century and before, all the more timely and necessary.

There's a bitter irony that, as Edmundson points out in her introduction, "women have long been associated with having supernatural powers and intuitive connections with the natural or supernatural worlds," yet this association is often seen, at least by men, as sinister or downright malevolent. Equally, while women might be considered creative they are rarely seen as—or perhaps more accurately, rarely allowed to be—innovative. Edmundson tells us that "the prevailing attitude of critics and the public in this period routinely denied women creative agency and asserted that women relied on adapting stories written by men in order to have their own work published." *Women's Weird* seeks to reject this attitude by showing how women not only "moved beyond the traditional ghost story"—blended their own, unique concerns into the weird form—but did so independently of men, sometimes ahead of them.

This is shown most clearly in Mary Cholmondley's "Let Loose." Cholmondley's tale is that of a keenly naive academic releasing an ancient evil from its prison in an "exceedingly dank" ossuary crypt, the story slowly building to a chilling and brutal climax. Without knowing any better, based on these narrative elements, a reader would likely assume the story owes a huge debt to the eerie work of M. R. James. Yet, as Edmundson reminds us, "Let Loose" was first published in 1890, fourteen years before James's *Ghost-Stories of an Antiquary*. Similarly, "Unseen—Unfeared" by Francis Stevens recounts the delirious experiences of Blaisdale and his meeting with an eccentric doctor who, through the means of a lamplike device and a South American "membrane," reveals the presence of previously unseen beings: "a huge, repulsive starfish," "centipedal things," and "sausage-shaped translucent horrors." This is immediately reminiscent of the "great inky, jellyish monstrosities" revealed by Crawford Tillinghast's "detestable electrical machine" in Lovecraft's "From Beyond." Yet "Unseen—Unfeared" was published in 1919, whereas "From Beyond" was written in 1920 and only published in 1934.

The content of the stories in *Women's Weird,* and the intent behind that content, is also powerfully different from the more male-dominated weird canon. Charlotte Perkins Gilman's "The Giant Wisteria," published the year before "The Yellow Wall Paper," uses a mere dozen pages to subtly investigate the persistent undermining of female agency by patriarchal systems. "The Haunted Saucepan," by Margery Lawrence, updates the traditional witch's cauldron into a modern domestic setting while also criticizing the condescending male attitude toward traditionally female tasks.

My favorite story from the anthology's thirteen tales is perhaps Mary Butt's "With or without Buttons." This blends all the elements of the weird—familiar objects made eerily unfamiliar, a force that reaches from beyond accepted reality, and the rapid loss of human control over events—into a dreamlike, lyrical prose:

> With every door and every window open, the old house was no more than a frame, a set of screens to display night, midsummer, perfume, the threaded stillness, the stars strung together, their spears glancing, penetrating an earth breathing silently, a female power asleep.

The contrast between ordinary and extraordinary events, the prosaic concern for decorum as that decorum is being corroded into panic, is masterful. Women's gloves, a symbol of delicacy and distance, become harbingers of a malevolent will. Scent bottles spray not sweet odors but repellent, mold-laced fumes. I found this a deeply affecting work and one that ended the anthology leaving me keen to search out more from both the authors included and their peers.

I should mention also the excellent presentation of this book by Handheld Press. The clean design, Edmundson's excellent introductory essay, a bibliography, and a very useful glossary all make this anthology stand out beyond peer works, even without consideration of its content.

Women's Weird is a valuable, important work in the study of weird writing. It is a powerful reminder that, despite what we may be told, artists and artworks are rarely lost but rather become forgotten, or even actively suppressed, when they don't fit the narratives of dominant cultural frameworks. Thankfully, we have scholars such as Melissa Edmundson reminding us that this writing still exists and showing how it is still relevant today.

A Trade in Futures
Daniel Raskin

"Surely, it is time for me to descend," utters the recluse. The weight of his undernourished body pressing against the cold damp aluminum slab on which he rests limits the function of his mouth and tongue, so that they lap and jiggle unconvincingly, producing a pitiable exhalation that deadens into the hiss-shriek of pipes that seep throughout his chamber. The fact of his breath's torpid annihilation into even this near, intimate space underscores to him the primal banality of his existence, and he is pleased to note this most recent synergy between himself and the world. It is one of few.

He dutifully arises, dresses in a gray smock, and shuffles toward the washtub, which delivers gray water from the commerce and distribution Complex under which he has sequestered himself, through an illegal tap. A system of screens and sumps filters the most conspicuous organic particulates, but is insufficient to clear the sour, clouded liquid that sluices into the basin. He submerses a soiled cloth into the murk and uses it to wet the swollen, puckered folds of his thighs and legs, which begin to quiver and pulse as the unknown solution is channeled to the raw membranes hidden within this recluse's intricate rash.

He raises his arm to insert a partially charged cadmium-ion battery into the socket-implant nestled between his ribs. This action is wet and numb. A weak voltage bleeds into the skin of his leg and reacts with the solution, which evaporates to a sickly vapor. This leaves behind a thin layer of substrate that rapidly changes form, first to a rough crystalline coating, and then to a viscous gel that is assimilated into the puckered, slaking walls of his rash through some organo-lithic innovation of metabolism, the nature or origins of which fails to pique even the slightest interest of the recluse, for whom this foul ablution represents nothing more than future earnings.

In this way, amidst the endless, sickening monotony of his

clammy chamber, the inflamed columns of his legs have patiently folded and pulsed into a truly abhorrent architecture. If one were to stare, and the recluse often did, the fractal latticework of pussing tissue would begin to appear as if it were masterfully sculpted to contain and conceal some abyssal void. Following the multitudinous pathways, one's eye would be drawn ever inwards toward the densest nests of putrid buttresses, sweating pilasters and yawning, microscopic loculi. Negative space could not be said to exist in this terrible mass, yet seeping from each fold, emanating from every pulse, is an unmistakable aspect of terrible negation. The leg-sculpture glows with it, infernally; it is a cage of the absolute.

"Ehh," grumbles the recluse. "By now, it must be worth something."

He locates a thin metal rod with a tapered end and uses it to scrape away the oily grit that has congealed around the edge of the access pipe hatch. It falls off in chunks. The effort exhausts him and he reflexively reaches down and shoves a handful of the grit into his mouth and swallows. This compulsion does not alleviate his exhaustion. Rather, the grit and its metallic grease excites his digestion and this discomfort stimulates him to carry on.

He opens the hatch and stumbles out of his chamber. The access pipe is a grimy, ill-used tunnel. Magnetized tracks hum stupidly as a barge drifts up the incline, hauling reams of clattering wreckage. When he first settled this sector of the Complex, the barges carried low-grade tailings from arche-civ mines in the outer provinces. His labors, thin and useless as they were, required him merely to whack off chunks of the mono-textural gray, blue, and dusty material that fell from the barge and haul them to his lair.

As he departs his chamber, he thinks of the last time he surfaced. He scavenged a pitted mass of epoxied wires for his bath. That he could distinguish different substrates within the tailings indicated to him a marked improvement in product quality. Reminded of this past acquisition, he pondered again its implications. Perhaps this represented new territorial acquisitions by the Complex, or perhaps some vicar had simply arranged for higher grades to ship through its favored routes.

Thinking about the vicars, a peevish grin—a grimace?—splits across his face. If he were to imagine them, which was something he was generally disinclined and perhaps even unable to do, he would have imagined a theater of dimly elegant silver face-things sitting court in a vast hall. Wires would splay taught out the heads of each of them, disappearing into the dark canopy of the hall. Within this silent and sinister court, machinations of power, intrigue and wickedness would emerge, resolve themselves with cold decisiveness and then dissipate, as the vicars' feuds and designs could only express themselves within the boundaries of the Complex's informational and energetic needs. The thing-faces, illuminated by pale blue light and buzzing silently, would never move, not once. In the absence of this imagination, the thought that spasmed in the recluse's mind was a simple fear-glee of not being seen, as vicars' awareness and interests generally pass over organics and other destitutes. As his cerebral glands exhausted their juices and expired, his grin-grimace fell and his face resumed its typically moldy resolution.

By the hollow vibrations in his ears he observes a barge drifting up the access pipe. He licks his fingers again to remind himself of the greasily blessed portal of his isolation, latches onto the barge car as it glides past and positions himself between the rails. The exertion of this maneuver taxes his legs even more than the previous effort of opening the hatch wore on his forearms. A dull pulsing courses up and down his legs, which he acknowledges primarily now as assets rather than mobility devices. The pain traces the subcutaneous sigils that determine the topographies of his rash. This sensation reminds him of squeezing tubes of the protein gel on which he has subsisted. He adjusts his body to ensure an adequate balance between security and something approaching comfort, and the recluse sinks again into the shiftless unfocus that has accompanied his long devotion. Time shrivels and contracts to fit within the flaking crevasses of his rash, and the barge courses upwards toward the Exchange terminus.

Dust and dry grit cakes his nostrils. The recluse coughs and spits himself into awareness as the barge jolts to a stop as it emerges from the access pipe. From his vantage, he sees a large tube lower itself from a far overhang that glows with a sickly and piercing light. He knows he must quickly extract himself from his position underneath the barge if he wants to avoid physical disintegration. From the tube, a thick liquid will ooze out, filling the barge container. The barge will then vibrate at a baffling intensity, inducing an exothermic coagulation of the liquid to the cargo, which is then offloaded into an unseen artery of the Complex as a luminescent blue gelatin. He has seen unfortunate organics fail to rise to the task of basic mobility as the Complex assimilates its scavenged metabolites. He does not know whether the vibration pulverizes or the heat incinerates, nor does he think on such terms, but he knows that he wishes to avoid this fate. The words that emerge in his mind are "I have these beauties to sell, so that I can descend rather than end." He rolls away from the barge, stumbles, crawls, and hobbles away from the barge, and he is able to create enough distance to avoid the surplus of violent energy that leaks from the Complex. He does feel, however, a kinship with this process by which matter is fused, energy expended, and a mystery is created. His legs quiver pleasurably as he watches the gelatin blocks float into the darkness.

Dare You Have Fun?

Fiona Maeve Geist

NICK MAMATAS. *Sabbath*. New York: Tor, 2019. 304 pp. $27.99 hc. ISBN: 978-1-250-17011-8; $16.00 pb (10/20). ISBN 978-1-250-17012-5.

A quick diagnostic for if you will enjoy *Sabbath:* do you like the idea of Nick Mamatas providing commentary on a *Hercules in New York*–style video game about hunting the seven deadly sins in modern Manhattan with occasional references to art, the art market, and contemporary politics? Does that sound like something you would relish the opportunity for? Or does it set your teeth on edge?

Mamatas seems to draw significant ire for holding polarizing opinions and, unsurprisingly, voicing them. This has drawn accusations of failed mimicry to describe his pastiche style—the unlikely but enjoyable hybrid of Beat culture and Lovecraftiana in *Move under Ground*—or, alternately, insufficient devotion to Lovecraftian kitsch in his Roman à clef *I Am Providence* (2016). Regardless, the most likely thing is that any fair reader would have a hard time denying Mamatas manages his stories with great adroitness. That is, he clearly introduces the critical elements of his plot, the relative stakes, and manages to have very kinetic, memorable, and somewhat unlikely scenes—the savaging of a (realistically battered) action hero by a trio of poodles remains something both surprisingly funny and oddly upsetting. The lashings of cosmic horror and rather wry commentary—especially when he happily lets himself go and be somewhat catty and venomous in a Evelyn Waugh–*Vile Bodies* sort of way. Ultimately, the crux of enjoyment for readers is if they believe that Mamatas is smug or clever—I personally find the author clever as a caveat for the remaining review.

Sabbath opens with a Jesse Bullington-esque (although somewhat more subdued) introduction to anti-hero Hexen Sabbath, who is happily humiliating his social superiors, wenching and failing to kill Danes for King and Country. In short succession Sabbath is informed that Danes aren't pagan, shows a moment of mercy, and is about to be fatally feathered with arrows when an Angel sprints him away to Manhattan to kill the Seven Deadly Sins (who are both personification and vehicles for critiques made via text). Sabbath is quickly, via hastily explained powers bestowed on this holy task, acclimated to New York and starts beheading sins: in *Highlander* fashion the sins must be decapitated. The ensuing fracas is quite bloody: Mamatas's fascination with combat sports is reflected in the clinical and professional presentation of armed and unarmed combat that anchors some of the more outlandish plot elements in a stark minimalist violence, giving the text an important weight that more cartoonish violence would undermine and making some impacts more squirm-inducing. If this appeals and, like me, you always wanted to watch an eleventh-century warrior be chased around by a *Wall Street* "Greed Is Good"–style monster, your very specific need is fulfilled. (It is possible you may have been previously unaware of this need.) The satirical delivery of a ludicrous story played straight is something admirable from my perspective; but, if you would like your eleventh-century warrior to be a typical anti-hero overcoming obstacles effortlessly and a more devoted focus on genre convention, it is probably something that you will feel much differently about.

    This is an important aspect to Mamatas's writing: he has a scabrous—particularly for a mainstream publication—sense of humor that is caustic to genre literature's tendency to take itself seriously, the somewhat disturbing fealty to a particular sort of grim fantasy in particular. Mamatas has a simultaneous mastery of genre conventions (the plot in the abstract is almost painfully standard) and utter distaste for them as expressed in sarcasm, scatology, sordid details, and the occasional bout of prolonged reflection or intellectual debate. The distrust expressed in the text for conventional narratives (of unlikely romance especially) being skewered and the text nearly begs the reader to argue with it. Arguably the gallery show (of seven canvases painted white) poses this question by their recurring inclusion (juxtaposed with the plot central seven deadly sins) which provide for extended commentary on why art is commercially valued and the actual difficulty of artistic creation (from even a purely mechanical standpoint). The responses to these paintings remains one of the strongest comedy beats in the story as a blood-soaked spree is occasionally reined in and a dinner party–style discussion between characters breaks out about the art exhibit itself. If you want a justification for why I come down in the positive evaluation camp: the smart dialogue, excellent plot timing, and enjoyable character studies that come from this plot beat (which could easily be a dusty stock trope explored frequently in the displaced as fish-out-of-water comedy beat that I associate with *Les Visiteurs* [1993]) are a demonstration of undeniable writing talents regardless of the merits of the storytelling itself—a somewhat self-assured performance of writer's craft.

However, from the practical non-theoretical and writer's craft perspective of the book market, *Sabbath* is still "fun" without reproducing stale genre parody tropes but rather exploring genre conventions without reverence and, occasionally, having *Rosencrantz and Guildenstern*–style fourth wall breaking to highlight the artifice. The adage that you really have to understand something to parody is legitimated by how *Sabbath* conforms to genre conventions in the abstract while the particular details of the plot undermine them—Sloth and Lust, the two least explored and ultimately least interesting and most genre-conformed and banal Sins, is where this starts ramping up—which lends itself to a certain florid maximalism.

Ultimately there's the time-honored knowledge that if sometimes someone shows up with a sealed pack of cards and after you've examined them offers to bet you that he can make the jack of spades leap from the deck and squirt cider in your ear, you *shouldn't* take the bet because clearly the other party knows something you don't. The bullet points of how this story should go are followed like pushpins in steady progression while simultaneously interrogating how these are received *as norms*. It's heady, you'll maybe want to argue with someone on the Internet about it—possibly Mamatas himself—but you won't have cider in your ear.

Dying to Meet You

Karen Joan Kohoutek

Playghoul: Special Vampira Issue. [New York:] Phantom Creep Theatre, 2020. 166 pp. No ISBN. $33.00. Limited to 666 copies.

Maila Nurmi, the artist and actress best known as the influential 1950s horror host Vampira, was a pioneer in the art of combining sex appeal with the macabre. Vampira is generally identified as the first television horror host, introducing and commenting upon older horror films in her costumed persona, three years before the syndicated *Shock Theater* collection of films led to the proliferation of local horror hosts such as Zacherley and Ghoulardi.

Despite her iconic status, there isn't a lot of substantial biographical material about Nurmi's life, apart from a few short documentaries and published references largely related to her work with Ed Wood, Jr. As a longtime Vampira fan, I was delighted to see that the Phantom Creep Theatre, a New York–based group known for its live spookshows, has published a tribute to Nurmi with the retro scrapbook *Playghoul,* a collection of articles published from 1950 to 1964.

Born in Finland in 1922, Nurmi grew up in the United States. A visual artist herself, she began a modeling career in the early 1950s, and her career in television was launched in 1954 with *The Vampira Show,* followed by a similar program simply called *Vampira* (1956). While neither series lasted longer than a year, she had a large following and active fan clubs, and her look of morbid glamour, with dramatic makeup, a long black wig, and a tight-waisted black gown, is immediately recognizable. She appeared in a few films, mostly in the Vampira character or some variation, receiving a level of notoriety with the cult film *Plan 9 from Outer Space* (1959). She died in 2008, at the age of eighty-five.

Playghoul's photo-packed, pre-browned pages tell Nurmi's story through vintage articles from the Hollywood press, representing magazines such as *Glamorous Models* and *Hush Hush,* as well as the more reputable *Life* and *TV Guide*. The articles follow Nurmi's arrival in California, as a model and cheesecake cover girl, to her tenure as Vampira, and later iterations. There is also a whole batch of tabloid coverage about her relationship with the doomed actor James Dean, and whether or not she put a "black magic" curse on him.

I am honestly surprised that it was possible to find so much of this material, given the ephemeral nature of popular magazines—they are rarely preserved—but it opens up a window into the reality of their times. I grew up hearing lots of jokes about women's measurements, 36-24-36 style, and now have real proof that the magazines did regularly and casually describe women that way. It was also interesting to note that, especially early in her career, the press frequently referred to the married actress as Mrs. Riesner, which seems oddly respectable, even formal, next to the accompanying glamour photos.

Most of the book is in black and white, but there's a splash of blood-red color in the transition to the Vampira era. After that point, the articles feature a lot of groan-worthy puns, a staple of the horror host genre, such as "local ghoul makes good" and the Beatnik-flavored "Real Gone Glamour Ghoul." Some of the ads from this era make me wish I could still join the fan club, care of the Coffin Case Co. in Venice, California, and get one of the original pins for *The Vampira Show*.

With its abundance of vintage material, this book could be enlightening for fans of mid-century style and pop culture, even if they have no particular interest in Nurmi. The strongest appeal, though, is obviously to Vampira fans, and fans of the Monster Kid phenomenon. A Goth aesthetic is created in front of us, with Nurmi's many prop-filled photo shoots: dancing on the beach wearing a bikini and a batwing cape, or posing in front of giant spider webs, a frothing potion in a martini glass. Nurmi also looks like an influence on punk style, in multiple photo shoots about shaving her head bald, with bangs and elaborate ear decorations, after a beauty parlor mishap.

Based on her PR pieces from the time, Nurmi seems to have always been candid about her ideas and motivations for the Vampira persona, talking about her love for horror films, especially their villains, and stating frankly about people, "I hate them. I expect people to be good and wise and kind and idealistic and they're not." Later, she attributes her appeal to the fact that "people have so much repressed evil they need a character to identify themselves with," particularly in providing an outlet for stifled youth.

Considering that Nurmi would sue Elvira for infringing on her character, it's amusing how openly she admits that the Vampira character was based on Charles Addams's drawings, later embodied in Carolyn Jones's Morticia. A few articles note that, within a year, there will be a blonde Vampira imitator named Voluptua, who has otherwise been almost completely forgotten in popular culture; and in one intriguing might-have-been, Nurmi talks about plans for a spin-off werewolf character to be called Wolverina.

The nature of the book, focused in time but wide in its scope, gives us a reminder that, in addition to her role as Vampira, Nurmi was a multifaceted visual artist, a "Young Girl with Ideas," as one headline called her. Even in her early modeling days, writers made frequent references to her eccentric, artistic nature, and as her career developed, she came across as a woman with great confidence in herself and in the Vampira character.

Playghoul is beautifully designed, with a gorgeous front cover by Donald David, of a busty Vampira posing on a pile of skulls. The book was offset printed and hand bound by the estimable Lance Thingmaker of Creepy Cult. In addition to the reprinted articles, it includes comics written by Phantom Creep member Mike Decay, illustrated by multiple artists, which combine spooky visuals and outer space themes, in homage to her *Plan 9 from Outer Space* days. It seems like faint praise to mention the table of contents, with dated, cited sources, and consistently used page numbers, but it's amazing how often those basics are missing from publications, and I never take them for granted.

The Nature of Horror

S. T. Joshi

RAMSEY CAMPBELL. *The Wise Friend*. London & New York: Flame Tree Press, 2020. 247 pp. $24.95/£20 hc (ISBN 978-1-78758-404-4); $14.95 tpb ISBN 978-1-78758-402-0; £9.95 tpb ISBN 978-1-78758-403-7.

In his long and distinguished career, Ramsey Campbell has exhibited a consuming interest in all the arts, not merely that of writing. It may not be known to many, but aside from his dozens of volumes of fiction, he is also a noted literary critic and an authority on film and (classical) music. These interests have found expression in some of his most powerful works. The number of writers in Campbell's novels and tales is legion, beginning with Errol Undercliffe, the purported author of two of the most harrowing tales in his early collection *Demons by Daylight* (1973). Another story in that collection, "The Franklyn Paragraphs," is one of the towering monuments of his entire corpus, where an author of horror fiction finds himself literally confronting the unspeakable. A lost film serves as the basis for the novel *Ancient Images* (1989). Campbell has devoted only a few works to the theme of music (such as the short stories "The Dark Show" and "No Strings"), but clearly music plays a significant role in his own life.

Campbell's new novel, *The Wise Friend,* is focused on pictorial art—specifically, the later paintings of a well-known artist, Thelma Turnbill, and their possibly supernatural impetus. As the novel opens, Thelma is already dead: she had either fallen, jumped, or been pushed from a tower block in the Liverpool area. The first-person narrator, Patrick Semple, is her nephew; and he has already been experiencing difficulty maintaining a connection with his fifteen-year-old son, Roy, following his divorce from his wife, Julia (who has custody of Roy). When Roy becomes fascinated with Thelma's paintings, just as Patrick had been when his aunt was alive, there seems to be the possibility of a tightening of bonds between father and son; but things take a very different turn as the novel progresses.

We receive only fleeting glimpses of Thelma's later life, when she divorced her longtime husband, Neville, and took up with a "companion" named Abel who became her "inspiration." We are also not given full particulars of the nature of Thelma's late work, aside from a passage early on that speaks of "how the intense lyricism of her early landscapes had grown hallucinatory before advancing into a highly personal form of surrealism, where enigmatic elements recalled the magical suggestions of Leonora Carrington, Thelma's favourite painter."

When Patrick and Roy begin visiting the places where Thelma had received inspiration for her paintings—especially Third Mile Wood, where they become momentarily lost and have difficulty finding their way out—the frequency with which disturbing details accumulate becomes unnerving. Consider this description of the wood:

> Already the trees looked flatter than they ought to be, more like a painting that could render us just as motionless. If they came to life I was afraid it might be a wrong kind. Perhaps they would start to dance where they stood, unless they scurried on their knuckly roots to clasp one another's branches before forming rings everywhere around us in a ritual dance. The holes fallen branches had left in the tree trunks looked about to gape if not to burst into song, to surround me with the lyric I'd heard last time we were here.

This proves to be a dream that Patrick had after his first visit to the wood, but it points to how the natural world, and the terrors it may conceal and then reveal, are really the focal point of the entire novel.

Things take a still more disturbing turn when Roy takes up with a girl, apparently of his own age, named Bella. At first, both Patrick and Julia are encouraged to see their son developing this relationship with a member of the opposite sex, but it is not long before Patrick finds this slight, enigmatic female (if indeed she is female, or even human) alarming and even terrifying. This sense of dread, nebulous at first, is substantially augmented when Patrick's parents die in a suspicious auto accident (Patrick was actually on the phone with them when the accident occurred) and, later, when a woman who had seen Thelma jump or fall off that tower block also dies mysteriously.

Meanwhile, Roy is becoming obsessed with Bella as only a fifteen-year-old can, and his father's objections only strengthen his resolve to stick with her. Patrick can only watch helplessly as Bella leads Roy to the various sites that Thelma had painted, collecting samples of earth just as Thelma herself had done (she had thrown them off that tower block just before her own death). And what of the fact that Bella's parents seem to be nowhere in sight, and that she apparently lives in an abandoned and derelict hotel? Patrick's own obsession with Bella—and his fervent desire to break her hold over his son—cause increasing tension with his son and his ex-wife, who makes the appalling suggestion that Patrick is sexually interested in her. But a book on witchcraft that Thelma had read—and that Roy and Bella had also pored over—tells Patrick more than he wants to know about who, or what, Bella really is.

The deceptively simple, even bland title of *The Wise Friend* masks one of the quiet triumphs in Campbell's novelistic output. With scarcely any overt horror until the concluding chapters, the novel incrementally creates a sense of *unease* that at times becomes almost unbearable. Patrick's wanderings through the wild, rustic areas that his aunt had painted lead his acute senses to discern the hideous possibility that the vegetation surrounding him has suddenly become sentient. His increasingly hostile dealings with Bella lead to sharp exchanges where every utterance augments the tension and dread. Early on, in a discussion of print books and their electronic counterparts, Bella states: "That's the way with old things. They come back in another form." Is she really talking about books here? In portraying her relationship with Roy, she says, "We're helping each other grow." Patrick and the reader suspect that there is far more to this than a trite expression of self-actualization.

Toward the end, when Patrick has unmasked Bella's true nature, she issues the ominous warning: "Expect me any time." Sure enough, Patrick now seems besieged—both at his home and his office, and all along the journey from the one to the other—with grotesque presences that she may have summoned up or that are various forms of her own identity. In an ambiguous conclusion, Patrick appears to have triumphed and saved his son—but we are left wondering if the horror is truly eliminated.

There is a great deal more to *The Wise Friend* than merely an excursion into age-old horror. I am particularly impressed at how Campbell has incorporated classical music—from Monteverdi to Britten—into the narrative, using these compositions at key moments to enhance the unnerving scenario. And Campbell's mastery at character portrayal is once again on display in his depiction of the increasingly frazzled Patrick, the naïve but headstrong Roy, and the embittered Julia, whose discussions with her ex-husband lay bare the contempt and loathing she feels for him. But it is Campbell's portrayal of the inscrutable Bella, who is clearly more than—or entirely different from—the fifteen-year-old girl she appears to be, that makes this novel the masterwork that it is.

We also must single out Campbell's richly textured, smooth-flowing prose. After more than fifty years of writing, Campbell has honed his prose idiom into a formidable weapon that can, with seeming effortlessness, say exactly what he wishes to say. Here, in a remarkable expansion of Poe's "unity of effect" to novel length, every single word has some bearing on the overall thrust of the narrative, and he can express fine shades of emotional resonance with the deftness of a Henry James without that author's occasional verbosity and turgidity. Campbell also has a bit of fun every now and then with contemporary usage, particularly the problematical use of "they" in the singular—which here causes all manner of ambiguities and confusions, just as it does in real life.

The Wise Friend may not have quite the spectacular horrific imagery of, say, *The House on Nazareth Hill* or the psychological intensity of *The Face That Must Die,* but it easily stands as a signal contribution to Campbell's oeuvre. Ramsey Campbell has already left nearly every other weird writer, past or present, in the dust; and this new novel only cements the lofty reputation he has achieved through a lifetime of stellar work.

Wisdom in Anguish: Sloane Leong's Dysmorphic Space Mechs

Helen Chazan

SLOANE LEONG. *With the Blade as Witness*. Carmichael, CA: Dim Shores, 2019. 50 pp. No ISBN. $12.00 tpb. Limited to 130 copies.

At least since a fit of road rage emboldened Go Nagai to envision a robot stomping across traffic in *Mazinger Z*, the giant robot has functioned as a sign of aggression, the (presumed masculine, presumed teen) id writ large and powerful, destructive personalities of steel and plastic. Unlike the similarly vibrant and fascist superhero, the super-robot is at once more and less knowable, somehow alive but clearly inanimate, filled with the hot consciousness of her pilot, rocket punching through Godzilla-like waves of rubble and obscene giant monsters. Koji Kabuto IS *Mazinger Z*; Koji Kabuto will never die; Kouji Kabuto dies in magma. A spirit goes in the robot, and that spirit just happens to always be a fighting spirit.

As in any mass genre ripe for reinvention, it would not be long until pessimism, inversion, and subversion transformed the genre's spirituality from within. Yoshiyuki Tomino's groundbreaking 1979 anime *Mobile Suit Gundam,* paradoxically the introduction of realistic machinery and psychic warfare to the genre, recast the mecha as an embodiment of war's consumption of the young. The Gundam RX0079 is a human tank, swallowing traumatized young pilots into her military breast. While the newly christened "real robot" genre continued to explore the possibilities of humanoid heavy machinery, a counter-tradition began to emerge in the fantasy-tinged designs of Yutaka Izubuchi's *Aura Battler Dunbine* and Mamoru Nagano's *Five Star Stories*. These robots are lithe and organic in their forms and eerily sensual with their impossibly slender, ornate, and sloping appendages. These wire mothers reached their generic apotheosis in Hideaki Anno and Ikuto Yamashita's *Neon Genesis Evangelion,* where the robot became womb and death chamber, emotionally crippled children immersed in amniotic fluid fused to the necks of gaunt monsters, their ferocious visage concealed almost comically under colorful shells.

It is this tradition of progressively erotic-grotesque media that *With the Blade as Witness* points us toward, and away from, in its opening pages. In our first encounter with the novella's Keepers, they are mysteriously fleshy, bestial abstractions/abjections:

> The moonlight hits the porous exangulous bone of his armored carapace, absorbing the luminance like water into sand and reflecting it out in a cool glow. His horned helm curves towards the sky, the shape of it an explosion of pale needles all tapering into the curve of a useless jaw, the sealed mouth forever locked into a long-suffering bite.

Something about this entity is staggering and godlike in an avenging, amoral sort of way—a werewolf the size of a planet. Is this a creature? A garment? A structure? An eldritch horror? Certainly, these geometries are not Euclidean, but there is something clearly seductive about the incomprehension such a description elicits. A reader could be forgiven for not recognizing that this description is of something fundamentally at least analogous to a giant mech, a towering humanoid warrior piloted by a human from within his breast. Any ambiguity is cleared up on the following page in an illustration of this mech by author/artist Sloane Leong.

Genre standards tell me to call such a thing a *mech,* but this being, called a Keeper by the culture of the planet where it stands, is more god than robot, totally baffling definition. The Keeper is fleshy, the Keeper is armored, but it is hard to say where the metal ends and the flesh begins. Are those wires or tendrils? Is his form fixed, like a giant knight, or is he fluid and mutable, a shifting presence? One thing is clear: the Keeper is massive. Crucially, the Keeper lacks one thing even the mysterious Units of Evangelion have: facial features. Instead, the mech's head, crowned with droopy, angular antlers, sports a vaguely clitoral shape. The Keeper's body is humanoid and familiar, but in that one spot we expect the certainty of anthropomorphism and emotional projection we are greeted with the blank mystery and obscenity of faceless genitalia.

These massive, mysterious entities are not exactly worshipped by the indigenous tribal cultures of the novella's seemingly alien world (it is hard to say that a world or culture is alien if it is not depicted existing in reference to our own world or indeed any larger defined network of other worlds). Rather, they are living instruments that fuse people, politics, and acts of worship in a sort of ritual mingling and arranged marriage. Their pilots, the Duelists, form a bond to the Keepers and battle other keepers in ritual combat, overtime withering away as their special connection to these great living, feeding suits of armor physically and mentally consumes them. The entire society is organized around this spectacle. It is a cruel blood sport perhaps, an endless sacrifice of young victims, but what it is not is endless war, no slaughtering strife with millions but a group betrothed to a life of unique, even transcendent pain.

The novella's protagonist, Vraya, is one such Duelist, a warrior lamb for the slaughter. Vraya is given no real choice—just like literal betrothal to an unknown fellow Duelist pilot of the Keeper Wisdom-in-Anguish, Vraya's bond to her Keeper Witness-to-Glory has been determined by her elders, denying her any sort of agency, any future beyond the belly of the beast. But something draws her to this connection. There's something beautiful, expressive, powerful in her connection to Wisdom-in-Anguish, a liberatory confusion between herself and the great body which becomes her armor. In her consciousness changing or is her body dying?

Sloane Leong tells stories about fragmented bodies and fragile, evolving identities, in a both a social justice and Cronenbergian sense. Working across media and genres, she is best known and deservedly acclaimed for her black-light textured, body-horror intersectional SF epic graphic novel series *Prism Stalker*. In and out of the fantastic, in words and in pictures, her work explores situations where the boundaries of cultural divisions are transcended and the often very physical angst that follows a life in such transgressions. In *With the Blade as Witness*'s fusion of the giant robot genre and science fantasy, Leong explores an intersection of gender dysphoria and post-colonial struggle—the pun of Duelist/Dualist may evoke for some readers the two-spirited gender expression found in North American Indigenous cultures. The Keepers themselves represent a fraught merging of painful trauma and the pleasure of transcending pain, both in the physical confusion of bodies and the symbolic, contradictory weight of their names: Witness-to-Glory's duelist is a witness to profound anguish, and the glory of Wisdom-in-Anguish is a knowledge of pain that the latter's duelist may not himself entirely comprehend. Pursuing ambiguities between dissociation and liberation, oppression and revolution, the novella is at once transcendent and sad, erotic and fatal. Leong does not imagine a better world, but she imagines one that is at once marvelously different and achingly familiar.

With the Blade as Witness is Leong's first novella-length prose story, and will likely invite comparisons to Ursula K. Le Guin and Octavia Butler, not only for her elliptical prose and provocative imaginary ethnography, but also because, unfortunately, it remains rare for literary SF to give marginalized race, gender, and sexual expressions much focus at all. Although Butler and Le Guin are clearly a valued, palpable influence on Leong's work, rather than taxonomizing her literary progenitors I'd rather end this review by turning back to the mecha anime designs I eulogized earlier. When we look at these fearsome, awesome, sexy, deathly designs, how can we begin to explain the dreadful wonder they inflict upon our gaze? Certainly the 30-minute anime programs that bore them could never hope to contain the full power of their titanic aesthetic. In her genre-warping novella, Leong has attempted the truly transformative and sought words worthy to match these unreal, impossible, living machines, these super robots. Removed from familiar cultural paradigms and reintroduced to our gaze with the benefit of the fear they really ought to have instilled all along, Leong leaves us with marvelous descriptions to match those designs, mechanical creatures that breathe and live.

Australia's Weird Poet Laureate

Leigh Blackmore

KYLA LEE WARD. *The Macabre Modern and Other Morbidities*. Edited by Charles Lovecraft. Illustrated by Kyla Lee Ward. Introduction by Dr Gillian Polack. Afterword by S. T. Joshi. Sydney: P'rea Press, 2019. 150 pp. $30.00 (AU) hc 978-0-9943901-3-4, $15.00 (AU); tpb ISBN: 978-0-9943901-2-7.

Confessing personal interest, I must first acknowledge that I have known Kyla Ward for around twenty-five years. The publication of her new book of poetry, *The Macabre Modern,* being her second volume entirely devoted to weird verse, places Ward in a unique position as Australia's most prolific writer of such verse. This is a niche position, but a meritorious one.

I would situate her work in the tradition of graveyard poetry represented by such poets as Thomas Lovell Beddoes. The mordant wit on display in her verse also recalls the work of Ambrose Bierce in such of his poetic collections as *Black Beetles in Amber* (1892).

However, Ward has her own distinctive voice. The esteemed American critic Winfield Townley Scott once remarked that "to scare is a slim purpose in poetry." Yet those of us who write such material realize that this is a simplistic approach to the matter. The Nobel Prize–winning novelist and playwright Samuel Beckett wrote that "We give birth astride a grave. The light gleams for an instant, and then it is dark once more." Work such as Ward's gives the reader the opportunity to contemplate the larger questions of life and death, to examine our own mortality.

The first section of *The Macabre Modern* treats of various dialogues between the figure of Death and people of various occupations, referencing the original Danse Macabre tradition. There is here, as well as weirdness and wonder, a delectable strain of black comedy. Ward appreciates the fine line, and indeed the frequent connection, between horror and humor

Ward's essay on the Danse Macabre is a valuable adjunct here to the reader's appreciation of her achievement.

But perhaps the strongest part of the volume is the second, featuring long poems, some of which verge on the epic. The poems here range across various cultures and ancient histories, from ancient Egypt through the Near East through to ancient China. These verses, both rhymed and unrhymed, are deeply imbued with insights gleaned from Ward's wide-ranging reading and knowledge. There are resonances of the macabre and the exotic. Ward frequently poses direct questions to the reader about their attitudes to life and death. The collection is rounded out with a suite of evocative illustrations by the poet herself.

The Macabre Modern is a piquant fusion of traditional and modern, an important addition not just to the poetry of the weird, but to Australian literature as a whole.

An Historical and Environmental Reading of August Derleth's "Ithaqua"

Edward Guimont

I have a confession: while I am a fan of Lovecraft and have extensively read both his works and scholarship on him, I have read very little writing by the other members of the Lovecraft Circle. Prior to this summer, outside of a few stories by Robert E. Howard and Clark Ashton Smith, I'm not sure I had read anything else save for "The Shadow out of Space" by August Derleth—a work I only read as research for a NecronomiCon presentation,[1] and which did not leave me greatly interested in reading anything further by him. To be fair, by that point I already had a preconceived dim notion of Derleth. I admired him (and still do) for arguably single-handedly ensuring the memory of Lovecraft became what it is today—but believed it came at the cost of diluting and obscuring the essence of Lovecraft, without any adding anything of true merit himself.

While I still believe that Derleth severely misunderstood Lovecraft, and to a major extent it was Derleth's version of Lovecraft that became popularized, I have slightly revised my belief that Derleth did not write anything Lovecraftian of value. While doing research for an article still in development, I read Derleth's stories about his Mythos deity Ithaqua. While the balance were unremarkable, I found the "Ithaqua" story itself to be surprisingly thought-provoking.[2]

A very brief and rough overview: "Ithaqua" was written in 1933, published in 1941, and is a sequel to Derleth's 1933

---

[1]. "At the Mountains of Mars: Lovecraft's Relationship with the Red Planet," presented at NecronomiCon 2017 and later adapted into an article for publication (Guimont).

[2]. In the collection *The Ithaqua Cycle*, Robert M. Price uses Derleth's original proposed title, "The Snow-Thing." I will continue to call the story by its published and better-known title, "Ithaqua."

story "The Thing That Walked on the Wind," though Derleth himself admitted it was close to a remake, being "patterned closely after" the earlier story (*ES* 601). The framing story of "Ithaqua" is a March 3, 1933 report by Constable James French of the Royal Northwest Mounted Police[3] to his division chief John Dalhousie at his headquarters in the (fictional) town of Cold Harbor, Manitoba. A French-Canadian priest, Father Brisbois, helps French investigate the disappearance of a man named Henry Lucas from the Navissa Camp along the old "Olassie trail." During the search, they find odd stone circles put out by the Native population. Lucas is discovered in the snow, apparently delusional with strange stories of having traveled to another planet. Ultimately, French warns Dalhousie that the Natives are planning to summon the entity Ithaqua using human sacrifices. Dalhousie plans to destroy the Native stone circles and suppress their worship—but to no avail.

In terms of writing quality, the prose is certainly serviceable, if not remarkable. The plot is interesting and does something different from, say, Derleth's follow-up "Beyond the Threshold," which is little more than an occasion to string along nouns and adjectives favored by Lovecraft. However, my main interest in the story is not so much the general plot itself but particular aspects of it—specifically historical, anthropological, supernatural, and environmental themes—that stuck out for me, and which I will address in turn below.

The first interesting characteristic of "Ithaqua" is a piece of historical information that Father Brisbois relates to French: "He asked me whether I had noticed that the Indians came from very old stock, probably Asiatic in origin. I admitted that I had noticed this. Then he said something about worship of gods old before man was born into the world" (75). The clear implication here is that the Natives of this area of Manitoba inherited their worship of Ithaqua from their ancestors back in Asia. As clearly stated as it is, as far as I can tell this thread by Derleth was only followed up by one author, Pierre Comtois in his 1985 story "Footsteps in the Sky." There, the main

---

3. Anachronistically, as the organization was dissolved and absorbed into the Royal Canadian Mounted Police in 1920.

character is New York City journalist Mathis Cordell, embedded in the Czechoslovak Legion during the Russian Civil War of 1917–22. When the Czechs attack a Siberian city and find its inhabitants dead or missing, some of the soldiers mention the name Ithaqua. Cordell recalls how he once covered a story in Canada where his guide, Monsieur Défago (from Algernon Blackwood's 1910 novella "The Wendigo") mentioned the legend to him. Cordell wonders if "Perhaps these beliefs were carried over from Asia to North America in prehistoric times across the Bering Sea land bridge" (Comtois 182–83).

There are two interesting things here in Brisbois's claims. The first is that the Natives of that region are "from very old stock, probably Asiatic." This seems to indicate that other Natives are *not* of Asian descent. While at the time the method of how the Paleoamericans emigrated to the Americas from Asia was still questioned, their Asian origin was not. However, the implicit division of Natives into older and younger "stock" by Derleth may have been his attempt to follow hints left by Lovecraft in several of his stories. In the 1918 tale "Polaris," the narrator has a dream of the distant future of the Arctic where both his civilization of Lomar and the Inutos that are its enemies have been displaced by the arrival of an apparently separate group, the "Esquimaux" (*CF* 1.69–70).[4] In "The Shadow out of Time" (1935), one of the time-displaced intellects with whom Peaslee speaks is "that of a king of Lomar who had ruled that terrible polar land 100,000 years before the squat, yellow Inutos came from the west to engulf it" (*CF* 3.398). The migration of the Inutos from the west (seemingly prior to that of the Esquimaux) would presumably be over the aforementioned Bering land bridge linking Siberia and Alaska, which was represented in an Elder Thing map of world in his 1931 short novel *At the Mountains of Madness* (*CF* 3.106).

---

4. Given the belief that "Polaris" was motivated by Lovecraft's feelings of powerlessness from being unable to enlist in World War I, and considering his fears of Japan later in life, this 'wave migration' concept possibly came from a fear that the war would destroy Western civilization and pave the way for Asian dominance in the future (perhaps also reflected by the sixth millennium dominance of the "cruel empire of Tsan-Chan" in "The Shadow out of Time" [*CF* 3.398]).

The use of the land bridge by Lovecraft is also notable, as it was not firmly established by science until the 1940s—indeed, after Derleth wrote "Ithaqua" as well.

The second interesting thing about Brisbois's (and Cordell's) claim is that the assertion that Native Americans maintained religious beliefs from thousands of years ago in Asia is actually prescient. The star cluster of the Pleiades and the constellation we know of as Ursa Major are both connected to folkloric beliefs originating in Central Asia up to thirty thousand years ago, and diffused across not only Eurasia, but northern Africa and across the Bering land bridge into the Americas. The belief in a northern bear constellation in particular has been cited as perhaps the oldest surviving human invention (Schaefer 98; Berezkin 80, 89).

Next to that timescale, the survival of a cult maintained by regular visitations of the gods themselves is certainly believable. However, the continuance of that long-preserved Native culture is placed in doubt at the end of the story. Constable French's final report to Dalhousie recommends

> that in the circumstances we would be quite justified in destroying these altars and issuing stern warnings to the Indians of Cold Harbor and the surrounding country. I have ascertained that dynamite is obtainable in the village, and I propose to go out and dynamite those hellish altars as soon as I have the proper authority from you to do so. (78)

Although French is unable to carry out his plans, Dalhousie nevertheless agrees with the course of action:

> There are even now rumors that Indians are gathering again for another meeting at the site of those accursed altars. That shall not and must not happen, and if they persist, they must be forcibly removed from the village and scattered throughout the provinces. I am going now to break up their hellish worship. (79)

The subsequent ending narration assures us that Dalhousie's plan was carried out: "The department scattered the Indians throughout the provinces, and all persons were forbidden to enter the forest bordering the unused Olassie trail" (79).

The concluding paragraph further refers to Ithaqua as "the god of the great white silence" (79). This a particularly apt term for this latest example of settler atrocity against Native culture and religion. Robert M. Price notes that stories involving Ithaqua worship tend to contain elements of postcolonialism, serving as an equivalent to revitalization movements like the Pacific Islander cargo cults and endorsing the efficacy of indigenous beliefs triumphing over white Western imperial oppressors with their Enlightenment beliefs (Price, "Wind" 200). While these movements among Native Americans in the United States, such as the 1890 Ghost Dance, were strongly suppressed by the American government, the process was initially different in Canada. As opposed to the U.S., the Canadian government imposed its will on the Western Natives only after the decline of both buffalo and Native populations. Natives in Canada were generally given the choice of "isolation or assimilation," and subjected to less intervention on tribal reservations than those in the U.S. Canadian policy was that the Natives were a dying civilization, and therefore the government's role was merely to watch over them until the final remnants either died off, or a few exceptional individuals had left their culture to join the settler community.

Because of this belief, Natives on Canadian reservations were left alone to practice their religious ceremonies without intervention well into the twentieth century. Indeed, the province of Manitoba itself was established as a result of the Canadian government broadly acceding to the demands of the indigenous peoples who revolted against Canada in the 1869–70 Red River Rebellion. This policy changed during the tenure of Duncan Campbell Scott (1913–32) as the chief administrator of the Canadian Department of Indian Affairs. It was under Scott that, beginning in the 1920s, the widespread expansion of the residential school policy occurred, with the specific aim of destroying Native culture and religion (Franks 234–38). In the context of "Ithaqua," therefore, the scattering of the Manitoba Natives to other provinces and the destruction of their cultural heritage and religious practice reflected the recent change to Canada's longstanding Native policy.

One can speculate that Scott's policies could, in the setting of "Ithaqua," have been used to provide cover for the suppression, in the same way that the U.S. government used Prohibition as a cover to disperse the residents of Innsmouth (*CF* 3.158–59). I should point out that in my own reading of Derleth's letters and nonfiction, I have not found any explicit references to Native Americans, and so his own view of them can only be speculated on.[5]

During the search along the Olassie trail, the party of heroes discover the body of Henry Lucas, the man who disappeared into the snow from his cabin in the middle of the night. Lucas is found apparently spun into a snow cocoon—but is not dead. In subsequent discussions with Lucas, Constable French begins to piece together what happened. Whispered voices from the sky had put Lucas into a hypnotic state, leading him out from his cabin in the middle of the night. In his own words, Lucas was then "carried away" by "something from above" before suffering what would now be called missing time. His next memory is standing in a stone circle in the midst of Natives worshipping a sentient green cloud among altars and fires. The cloud began to descend, with Lucas finding himself (metaphorically) frozen in place, unable to flee, before the cloud lifted him up into the air again. In the words of French, "After that, his story is by no means clear. We can gather that he was taken somewhere—either far underground or far above the earth. From some of the phrases he let drop, we might suspect that he had been on another planet, were this not absolutely impossible." The truth remains out there for French, as Lucas dies from exposure three hours later (76–77).

The story of Lucas and his abduction by Ithaqua jumped out to me for the fact that a number of details from his account seem prescient to abduction tropes that emerged more than three decades after Derleth wrote the story. In his introduction to Chaosium's *The Ithaqua Cycle* collection, Price not-

---

5. Although not involving Derleth himself, I was interested to find that Richard A. Fawcett, founder of the August Derleth Society, was from Uncasville, Connecticut—a town named after the Mohegan sachem Uncas, and the location of the Mohegan Nation tribal reservation (Fawcett ii).

ed that Derleth was attracted to the Fortean aspect of the "Fishers from Outside," also used by Lovecraft in such stories as "Winged Death" (*CF* 4.348). Charles Fort's belief was that entities beyond our world would, for amusement or more inscrutable reasons, catch humans, look them over, and (sometimes) toss them back, much as an amateur fisherman might. If this sounds somewhat familiar, it is because, to quote Price, "In our day, this idea has become the central premise of a virtual religion of self-fancied UFO abductees." (Price, "Introduction" xi). Brian Lumley expanded on this concept in his 1978 novel *Spawn of the Winds*, establishing that Ithaqua took his victims to the planet Borea, where an entire population of those descended from Earth's various Arctic cultures resides (42–43).

Reading "Ithaqua," I felt that Price's almost offhand comparison between Derleth and alien abduction accounts was underselling the striking parallels in the story. It has been more common to trace, as critic of pseudohistory Jason Colavito has extensively done (and as Price himself earlier noted with Charles Garofalo as far back as 1982), the extent to which Lovecraft inspired ancient alien claims. However, anthropologist Jeb J. Card has also pointed out that many of the alien abduction tropes that became established in the 1980s can be found in "The Whisperer in Darkness."[6] "Ithaqua" also has strong abduction trope elements in it; what is more, they are different from those in "Whisperer," making it clear that Derleth was not just copying aspects from a Lovecraft story into his own. In particular, while many features of Lucas's story have abduction elements—even the worshipping Natives can be seen as a parallel to abductees claiming to see aliens

---

6. Prominent cryptozoologist Loren Coleman has noted that there are a number of notable cryptid sightings in New England featuring beings with bulbous heads, such as the Melon Heads of Connecticut and the Dover Demon of Massachusetts. Combined with Card's claims on "The Whisperer in Darkness," one also wonders if the alien abduction trope—established with the 1961 Betty and Barney Hill abduction in New Hampshire—should be seen as an outgrowth of New England folklore, at least before it became a more widespread and standardized phenomenon in the 1980s. This avenue of thought is beyond the scope of this review but is deserving of future study.

busy with their own tasks while they are unable to move—aspects like being taken underground and the use of hypnosis, telepathic voices from above, and the underground captivity are evocative of elements common in the "Shaver Mystery," a series of articles originating in the science fiction magazine *Amazing Stories* in 1945. In the late 1940s, the proponents of the Shaver Mystery, Richard Shaver and Ray Palmer, would help establish modern UFO lore, and the Mystery itself heavily drew on Lovecraft (Warner 180–85).

Palmer was from Milwaukee, and both he and Shaver lived in Wisconsin during the late 1940s when they were incorporating the Shaver material into the emerging UFO field. While a direct influence on them by Derleth remains hypothetical, if intriguing, it does show that in "Ithaqua" Derleth at the very least anticipated a new development that would arrive in both speculative fiction and in reality nearly fifteen years after he initially wrote the story. While the Shaver link remains notional, there is one feedback loop very thematically prominent in "Ithaqua"—that of the environment and its impact on humanity.

In "Ithaqua," the namesake god serves as an embodiment of the fear that humanity will eventually be doomed by irrevocable change to Earth's climate. But instead of the heat of global warming, the change represented by Ithaqua is that of advancing cold. "Ithaqua" was written at a time when it there was a general belief the Earth would eventually die from freezing as the sun burned out. Stellar fusion was not fully accepted by the scientific community until the late 1930s, and as such, the lifespan of the sun was estimated to be far shorter than current astronomical beliefs. This seemingly scientific fear of the Earth's frigid fate was, of course, depicted in science fiction works set in the future. One prominent example was William Hope Hodgson's *The Night Land* (1912), cited by Lovecraft in "Supernatural Horror in Literature" (*CE* 2.115); Hodgson was also an influence on Derleth (Howard 56). "The Shadow out of Time" also has the Earth winding up as a frozen wasteland in the distant future (*CF* 3.399–400). I have noted before that in his sequel story "The Shadow out of Space," Derleth seems to have either forgotten or misinterpreted this (Guimont 56). To be charitable to Derleth, "The Shadow out of Space" was published in 1957, and he may have incorporated later astronomical research into it, although his science fiction was often filled with basic astronomy errors (Howard 55).

If Derleth had forgotten the cold fate awaiting humanity in "The Shadow out of Time," the fear was still evident in "Ithaqua." At the start of the story, the Canadian public is left in quiet dread of "a strange god of the great white silence, the vast land where snow lies for long months beneath a limitless, cold sky" (69), seemingly a vision of the entire world that awaits if it falls under the dominion of Ithaqua. This dread spreads "by means of a strange grapevine system of communication, apparently not by word of mouth, since no one was ever heard to speak of it" (69)—a reluctance to acknowledge the true severity of the climate crisis that is all too recognizable in the twenty-first century. It is by paths of footprints in the snow, and their sudden vanishing, that the victims of Ithaqua are followed and identified (70–73). Ithaqua itself leaves footprints that turn the snow into an unnatural form— "like glass, smooth, but not slippery" (72)—transmuting the element he is most associated with into an otherworldly incarnation. When Constable French becomes convinced that he is being stalked by Ithaqua along the Olassie trail, he feels "the fear that the thing that encompassed me was all around me in the falling snow. For the first time in my life I was afraid of . . . the silent snow" (74). When Lucas is found, he is "cold as the stones in the circle I had touched, and the body was wrapped in a cloak of spun snow" (76). Lucas dies shortly thereafter, his body never able to regain its proper temperature despite being attended by Dr. Telfer (76–77).

In "Ithaqua," therefore, there is a theme of coldness bringing death. But beyond that, Ithaqua the god has the ability to give new fears to cold, and to change its very nature. It is not ice that traps Lucas or threatens French's return; it is fluffy snow. Lucas, having been touched by Ithaqua, is beyond the reach of modern science to restore warmth to. And of course, the center of Ithaqua's worship is none other than the town of Cold Harbor (71–72)—the word "harbor" carrying a connotation of arrival from elsewhere. Ithaqua itself is that cold, arriving to Earth from beyond. The fate of Henry Lucas is the ultimate fate of all humanity.

I started reading "Ithaqua" with a mix of trepidation and resignation, especially as it initially seemed to be a retreat of "The Thing That Walked on the Wind." By the end of the story, my negativity had fully evaporated. In preparation for this article, I read some of Derleth's nonfiction for the first time, and enjoyed his observations of his town and world and the people inhabiting it—an even further cry from the secondhand Cthulhu Mythos stories I had associated with him. While I doubt the majority of Derleth's stories will provide as much food for thought as "Ithaqua," I am now at least interested in reading them, and far more interested in reading more of (and by) Derleth the man. This conversion more than anything shows the true cosmic power of the frozen god Ithaqua.

Works Cited

Berezkin, Yuri. "The Cosmic Hunt: Variants of a Siberian–North-American Myth." *Folklore* 31 (2005): 79–100.

Comtois, Pierre. "Footsteps in the Sky." In Robert M. Price, ed. *The Ithaqua Cycle: The Wind-Walker of the Icy Wastes: 14 Tales*. Hayward, CA: Chaosium, 2006. 170–86.

Derleth, August. "The Snow-Thing" [i.e., "Ithaqua"]. In Robert M. Price, ed. *The Ithaqua Cycle: The Wind-Walker of the Icy Wastes: 14 Tales*. Hayward, CA: Chaosium, 2006. 69–79.

Fawcett, Richard A. "Middle America in Amber: An Introduction." In James P. Roberts, ed. *Return to Derleth: Selected Essays*. Madison, WI: White Hawk Press, 1993. i–ii.

Franks, C. E. S. "Indian Policy: Canada and the United States Compared." In Curtis Cook and Juan D. Lindau, ed. *Aboriginal Rights and Self-Government: The Canadian and Mexican Experience in North American Perspective*. Montreal: McGill-Queen's University Press, 2000. 221–63.

Guimont, Edward. "At the Mountains of Mars: Viewing the Red Planet through a Lovecraftian Lens." In Dennis P.

Quinn, ed. *Lovecraftian Proceedings No. 3*. New York: Hippocampus Press, 2019. 52–69.

Howard, John. "Somebody Pointed Earth: August Derleth's Science Fiction." In James P. Roberts, ed. *Return to Derleth: Selected Essays, Volume Two*. Madison, WI: White Hawk Press, 1995. 53–59.

Lovecraft, H. P. *Collected Fiction: A Variorum Edition*. Ed. S. T. Joshi. New York: Hippocampus Press, 2015–17. 4 vols. [Abbreviated in the text as *CF*.]

———, and August Derleth. *Essential Solitude, The Letters of H. P. Lovecraft and August Derleth*. Ed. David E. Schultz and S. T. Joshi. New York: Hippocampus Press, 2013. [Abbreviated in the text as *ES*.]

Lumley, Brian. *Spawn of the Winds*. New York: Jove, 1978.

Price, Robert M. "About 'The Wind Has Teeth.'" In Robert M. Price, ed. *The Ithaqua Cycle: The Wind-Walker of the Icy Wastes: 14 Tales*. Hayward, CA: Chaosium, 2006. 200.

———. "Introduction: Ghost Riders in the Sky." In Robert M. Price, ed. *The Ithaqua Cycle: The Wind-Walker of the Icy Wastes: 14 Tales*. Hayward, CA: Chaosium, 2006. ix-xii.

Schaefer, Bradley E. "The Origin of the Greek Constellations." *Scientific American* 295 (2006): 96–101.

Warner, Harry, Jr. *All Our Yesterdays: An Informal History of Science Fiction Fandom in the Forties*. Chicago: Advent, 1969.

Cosmic Horror—with a Dash of Sex

Gary Fry

S. T. JOSHI. *Something from Below*. Hornsea, UK: PS Publishing,, 2019. 127 pp. £18 hc. ISBN: 978-1-786363-80-0; £25. Signed hc. 978-1-786363-81-7.

S. T. Joshi has spent the great majority of his career commenting upon and editing/publishing work focused on cosmic horror, with only the occasional foray into writing any himself. But now we have a novella squarely located in that (other)world, so I guess we need to ask, given Joshi's analytical expertise in this subgenre, whether he can pull off the same standard of material in a fictional sense.

The book opens with Alison Mannering returning to her native town shortly after her father's death. Her father worked at a local mine, the main source of employment in the area, and there are suspicious circumstances involved in his demise. Cue Alison's investigations into recent events, all of which draw her inexorably down into the mine itself.

The author is good at establishing character, his first-person narrative convincing in its details of a woman seeking reintegration into the locality of her youth. The friction with her mother, reacquaintance with an old boyfriend, and then ad hoc sleuthing are all conveyed in a highly readable prose with more than a dash of style about it.

The novella unfolds at a steady pace, with a familiar string of developments. After accessing information from old newspapers at a local library, Alison conducts inquiries with the spouses of other men who have died at the mine, before becoming aware of the business's nefarious owner, whose ultimate appearance is pleasingly counterintuitive. Yes, he's the villain of the piece, but not quite in the way similar fictions might lead the reader to expect. I found this a pleasing twist in a piece that felt for the large part conventional. Indeed, the last quarter transforms the whole, though hints of its subversive nature have been present all along.

Indeed, Joshi strays into potentially controversial territory when he reveals the methods to which Alison resorts in order to manage her investigations. This involves sexually manipulating her former boyfriend, a development that some readers will interpret as her being willfully independent and others might consider rather typical of a male author. All the same, given the novella's denouement, this focus on sexuality is required, and whether it is justified will depend on how each reader interprets that conclusion.

Myself, I found it both pleasing in a traditional cosmic horror sense and reticently suggestive of gender politics. The piece certainly turns out to be more ambitious than any number of other Lovecraftian pieces in which the "thing" stands for nothing more than an otherworldly entity, however effectively conveyed. Joshi's provocative central character, and the moral dilemma she ultimately faces, will probably divide the field's community, but rather that than the "safe" horror I see so often and find tiresomely unmemorable.

Overall, I greatly enjoyed this lengthy novella and read it in a single sitting, at first settling into its cozy familiarity and then feeling rattled by that edgy ending. A few minor issues struck me, mainly lapses in the author's style. Amid original and incisive paragraphs, I found such stock phrases as "snoring her head off" and "stopped in my tracks" and, worst of all because these appear within the space of several lines, "bigger fish to fry" and "taking the bull by the horns." Here we have missed opportunities to make the prose shine. Joshi also seems enamored of the (unusual) word "mulishly," as it appears several times in the novella, but that really is being overly fussy.

What we have here then is a striking addition to the cosmic horror subgenre, one that's bound to divide readers, particularly, I feel, during this period of high-stake gender politics, the so-called "male gaze," and issues of fictional appropriation. All this constitutes the broader cultural context into which Joshi releases his novella, but nobody could ever accuse him of shying away from potential controversy or of being boring. I truly admired this work, and what that says about me can only be decided if you buy and read the book.

Providentially Speaking Again
Donald Sidney-Fryer

T. E. D. KLEIN. *Providence After Dark and Other Writings.* New York: Hippocampus Press, 2019. 591 pp. $30.00 tpb. ISBN: 978-1-61498-268-5.

During the year 2019 it has happened as my great good fortune to have reviewed three or four major publications from Derrick Hussey and his Hippocampus Press, both of which now seem as magical and numinous as August Derleth and his Arkham House. All this, plus the ongoing and abundant volumes of the Lovecraft correspondence. First at my request there came from designer David E. Schultz a proof copy of Leah Bodine Drake's *The Song of the Sun,* her collected writings, at 760 pages, as largely and quite capably assembled and edited by Master Schultz. Second, Arthur Machen's *Collected Fiction,* impeccably assembled and edited by S. T. Joshi, in three volumes; and a fourth volume of critical writings edited by Messieurs Mark Valentine and Timothy J. Jarvis; all four volumes totaling 2056 pages. Third, D. L. Myers's exceptional first volume of poetry, *Oracles from the Black Pool,* published like Klein's own much larger book in October 2019, but in Myers's case at 136 pages, which I review elsewhere, and quite positively—richly deserved.

The point that I am highlighting here? At 37 lines per page, whether prose or poetry, all these identified books constitute a considerable amount of discourse liberated for creative purposes. These publications, including the latest (by Ted Klein), represent strategic or important landmarks in the annals of modern imaginative literature, much of it speculative prose or poetry; as if all fiction is not in one sense speculative, even if nominally dealing with common reality.

Ted Klein is indeed a special case with his two classics of modern fiction, the novel *The Ceremonies* and the collection *Dark Gods.* Although never attested in print (in anything I have seen), Klein is a professional writer, a journalist writing for newspapers and magazines, like many of my favorite poets and prosateurs, including L. B. Drake, Louis Bertrand, Arthur Machen, or Margaret Munnerlyn Mitchell for that matter. In other words, Klein is a practiced and more than merely competent author; and it clearly shows in this exceptional tome of his collected essays now set before me.

On this opus I have spent a week carefully perusing it before committing pen to paper. A small note after the contents pages but before the official "Author's Note" informs me that, although Klein is in fact the author, S. T. Joshi is the instigator-assembler-editor of the collection. Therefore I have neatly written on the title page (where it should stand in print), an inch or so below the author's name, "Edited by S. T. Joshi." And as the back cover states in all truth, the compilation is indeed notable for "covering a remarkably wide range of topics with elegance and wit," a collection in which Klein in fact "reveals his skill as an essayist and reviewer," and impressively so.

In the current flux of publications emanating from Hippocampus Press, the author finds himself in distinguished company, some of them the literary objects of his fervid youthful admirations (or connected to them), Lovecraft, Machen, and Ramsey Campbell, among others. The titles of the six sections into which Joshi has ordered this gallimaufry of materials indicate these early but continuing enthusiasms: I. On Lovecraft; II. On Other Authors; III. *The Twilight Zone;* IV. On Film; V. On Other Topics; VI. Reviews. A nice and reassuring touch: each section ends with some earnest writer or reporter interviewing Klein, whereby we learn much about him and his literary output.

Among other activities he has edited several magazines including *The Twilight Zone* and *CrimeBeat*. He has had op-ed pieces published in the *New York Times,* the *Washington Post*, and so forth, a pretty impressive record.

The collection contains an incredible spectrum of intelligent and informed commentary on all manner of subjects, authors, books, magazines, etc., and not only topics in the genre of supernatural horror. This reviewer finds that he shares many predilections with Klein, not just favorite authors like

Machen but (big surprise!) poetry above all. In addition to manifesting himself as a quite knowledgeable poetry connoisseur, or poetry consumer (his phrase), he is also a remarkable poet himself, as witness "Lament of an Aging English Instructor," but especially "The Book of Hieronymus Bosch"—an exceptional sestina on the grand scale laid out on two adjoining pages almost at the exact center of the collection. This is a masterpiece wherein Klein expresses something essential about Bosch and the human (or inhuman) condition. This sestina results in something as important as any or all the prose in *Providence After Dark*.

How much have I learned from this compilation! Not just about literature and its creators (mostly nineteenth and twentieth centuries), films and their makers, but so much that I did not myself see during the 1970s, 1980s, and 1990s, when I preoccupied myself with workaday jobs or just plain existing. I cannot even begin to broach the myriad subjects addressed in *Providence After Dark*. Klein speaks out forthrightly against the abuse and murder of animals as literally perpetrated by the new breed of movie-makers, signalized in two essays at the start of section IV. I also learn that, according to modern physicist Lawrence M. Krauss, the cosmos possesses some 100 billion galaxies at large, and that each galaxy contains about 100 billion stars. No speculation or discussion in this estimate concerning about how many planets major or minor may or may not exist relative to all these galaxies and stars!

For me the single most entertaining section is the extended "Sci-Fi Entertainment," as amazing, unprecedented, instructive, and, on occasion, hilarious as any other section or article. The mention of Portmeirion in western Wales (anent the British television series *The Prisoner*), with its rhododendron plantation, caught me by real surprise. Machen would have known and cherished this extremely picturesque town and ambiance. Many people came to know of this place only because its use as the locale for a television series.

Whatever Klein uses as his topic or subject, he writes very well and entertainingly. We heartily recommend this collection by one Ted Klein, journaliste extraordinaire.

A concluding aside, lest we forget.

We wish to speak out on something, a verbal usage, easily observable in Klein's abundant compilation, and in many other books and articles dealing with supernatural horror. It lies in the word or term of horror, as aligned with that of terror.

Whether writers or readers of horror fiction, or spectators of horror movies, such people are obviously aficionados of modern fantasy, science fiction, science fantasy, however we define these terms. They all form part of speculative literature.

Such aficionados do not generally confuse such stories with tales of pure physical grue, as in a story or history of murder or wanton or systematic killing. We refer here to the clandestine and willful extermination by the Nazis of Jews, Gypsies, and other minorities in the death camps located mostly in Poland. In these death camps the Nazis murdered some six million people, an awesome total.

However, when we think of all these millions as individuals, we contemplate an infinite number of real horror stories. Those victims—who, until the last moment, naked in the gas chambers, still held on to their innocent belief in the Nazi promise of their being resettled in some other location—would have known that last moment as one of total horror and terror combined, when the doors to the gas chambers closed and could not be opened from the inside. These are all tales of horror that we should not forget, albeit different in kind from the tales of supernatural horror.

The story of supernatural horror, as both directly and implicitly defined by him in many of the essays gathered in *Providence After Dark,* Klein beautifully exemplifies in his own fiction, *The Ceremonies* and *Dark Gods*. Machen himself exemplifies it in the novel *The Terror,* about the animal kingdom rising up and attacking humans because of their abandonment of spiritual or supernatural beliefs and values, especially as provided by many of the organized religions. The Welsh author also beautifully exemplified it in a story of the radiant and numinous, the novelette "The Great Return," about the return of the Holy Grail, the Sangraal. Thus in a sense the tale of supernatural horror might be interpreted not just as the desire of writers and readers to give themselves a good scare, a great fright, but as a desire toward religion, not necessarily organized religion (no disrespect to the institution), but as an universal need vis-à-vis the physical cosmos.

Despite what Lovecraft states in "Supernatural Horror in Literature," we have never found Machen to be that echt-cosmic in his fiction as displayed at least in some blatant manner. George Sterling, Ashton Smith, or Lovecraft himself are more demonstrably cosmic-minded, or cosmic-astronomic-minded. Nonetheless, however manifested, Machen remains a Titan of the Supernatural.

Some of Your Blood:
Dracula's Metafictional Mirror

Philip Challinor

Most readers of Theodore Sturgeon's 1961 masterpiece *Some of Your Blood* will have noticed that it shares its epistolary format with Bram Stoker's *Dracula* (1897). However, the relationship between the two books goes considerably further than that. In various aspects of its plot and characterization, the later novel both resembles and reverses its predecessor. More unconventionally, the prologue and epilogue of *Some of Your Blood* provide a disturbing frame for the vampire's mirror image.

Leaving aside the prologue and epilogue for the moment, *Some of Your Blood* presents itself as the case file of a young American soldier's psychiatric treatment at a military clinic. The soldier, who punched a major during a scuffle and, apparently for no better reason than the officer's vindictiveness, was detained for months as violent and dangerous with an unclassified psychosis. When the major dies in a plane crash, Colonel Williams transfers the young man to the care of Dr. Outerbridge, a trusted friend and subordinate, asking him to arrange an expedient medical discharge that won't reflect badly on the army. At Outerbridge's request the young man writes down the story of his life, using the third person and the pseudonym "George Smith" as aids to objectivity. He produces a lengthy (approximately half the book) and vivid account of his poverty-blighted rural background as the son of a violent alcoholic; his love of hunting in the forest; and his sexual involvement with a young woman named Anna. He also mentions a term in the reformatory, where the order and cleanliness contrasted very favorably with his life at home; and his eventual enlistment in the army when Anna became pregnant.

This document, along with subsequent conversations and psychological tests, convinces Outerbridge that despite appearances Smith is indeed seriously disturbed and potentially violent. As Colonel Williams becomes impatient to see the case wrapped up, Outerbridge confronts Smith with what he has deduced: that when suffering emotional stress and turmoil Smith has a compulsion to drink blood. Under hypnosis, Smith details several killings "hidden in plain sight" in his autobiography, and Williams sends a nurse, Lucy Quigley, to Smith's home town to investigate. Quigley verifies Smith's account, and the file ends with the document that started the whole affair when it attracted the attention of an army censor who showed it to the major: a brief yet intensely emotional love letter to Anna.

Both *Dracula* and *Some of Your Blood* are contemporary in setting, and both (with a significant exception to be considered later) emphasize their up-to-date realism: *Dracula* with modern technology like Dr. Seward's phonograph, *Some of Your Blood* with its focus on modern psychiatric techniques such as the Rorschach test, and both with their documentary narratives telling the story purportedly via primary sources.

George Smith's real first name is Béla (Anna calls him Belly), which presumably means his forebears were Hungarian. Although Smith writes only that his parents came from "the old country," Transylvania has a large Hungarian minority that includes Székely, the ethnic group to which Stoker's count was proud to belong. During Jonathan Harker's visit to his castle, Dracula uses their conversations to improve his English pronunciation so that he can blend in better with the natives when he emigrates; Smith, the son of immigrants, is initially bullied by other children because of his "honky talk," but quickly learns to speak American English like everyone else.

Dr. Van Helsing compares Dracula to a habitual criminal, intelligent but psychologically handicapped by a combination of ignorance and inflexibility: "This criminal has not full man brain. He is clever and cunning and resourceful, but he be not of man stature as to brain. He be of child brain in much." Dr Outerbridge and Nurse Quigley both diagnose Smith's emotional state as being "arrested at the lowest levels of infancy," despite his full physical development and the high level of native intelligence and verbal ability demonstrated in his autobiography.

The inversions are as neat as the parallels. Dracula is wealthy, aristocratic, ancient, and supernatural; Smith is poor, a commoner, youthful, and non-supernatural. In life, Dracula was a successful and ruthless military leader; Smith joins the army as an enlisted soldier and is traumatized at the sight of casualties—though not, as becomes clear, because he is particularly squeamish about violent death. While Dracula's bloodlust is for women, Smith's is less discriminating. He does use his girlfriend Anna as a source of blood, but he also uses a young boy, an alcoholic watchman, and a wide variety of animals.

Dracula is structured as a thriller: the Count's evil nature becomes evident to Jonathan Harker in the opening chapters, and most of the story consists of move and counter-move between clearly defined opponents, climaxing in a chase and unequivocal victory for the forces of Christian virtue. *Some of Your Blood* is structured as a "fair-play" detective story whose clues are ingeniously embedded in Smith's tour de force of an autobiography. There is no climactic chase, as the book begins with Smith already incarcerated at the clinic; and for much of its length there is some doubt as to whether Smith has really done anything worse than accidentally strike an officer. Smith's autobiography convinces Williams that Smith's "only sickness is scar tissue from a regrettable childhood" and that he has "placed sex in a genuinely wholesome perspective," and most first-time readers would probably agree. More sensitive than Williams to the peculiarities and omissions in Smith's narrative, Outerbridge is able to retain his focus on the basic problem of the case: the real motive behind Smith's hunting.

Dracula has no omniscient narrator, and the diaries, letters, and memoranda and their authors are indicated with plain headings: "Jonathan Harker's Journal," "Dr Seward's Diary," and so forth. *Some of Your Blood* has an anonymous narrator who provides the prologue and epilogue, and who also continually appears between the documents in the file, identifying them with headings such as "Here is a letter" and "Here is the answer," or simply "A letter." The narrator also explains the psychological tests that Outerbridge uses on Smith, and at one point intercedes to remind the reader of the doctor's situation "on the struggling staff of an overcrowded, underequipped military neuro-psychiatric hospital." The narrator's voice is one of the most intriguing features of *Some of Your Blood,* not least because it begins by telling us to disbelieve what we are reading.

Sturgeon opens his story with an explicit assertion that its characters and events are fictitious. Paradoxically, the denial of realism is couched in solidly realistic terms: the reader is not depicted as simply floating above the action to observe events, and is not merely told to sit back and imagine. Instead we receive detailed instructions to use a key, climb a flight of stairs, turn left for the study, open a drawer, and take out the file containing the records of Smith's case. The reason all this is possible: "you are The Reader, and this is fiction. . . . You're quite safe."

This reassurance, and the next (and last) sentence of the prologue, "It is, it is, it really is fiction . . ." provide a blatantly false sense of security. Why should it matter so much that what we are about to read is fiction, like the Dr. Outerbridge whose own non-existence will conveniently prevent his objecting to our burglary of his study? The epilogue continues in the same vein, repeating that Outerbridge "exists only for you, The Reader" and proclaiming that "this is and must be fiction." The "must be" is ambiguous: it could mean that the story is inherently implausible, even impossible, or it could mean that the story is so horrifying that the possibility of its truth cannot be admitted.

This is rather more complex and disturbing than Stoker's double-bluff at the end of *Dracula,* where Jonathan Harker notes both the story's implausibility and the unreliability of the written record: "in all the mass of material of which the record is composed, there is hardly one authentic document. . . . We could hardly ask any one, even did we wish to, to accept these as proofs of so wild a story." Harker quotes Van Helsing's "We ask none to believe us," but the narrator in *Some of Your Blood* goes further and actively solicits—in places virtually begs for—our disbelief. If confined to the prologue, all this might be seen as an authorial trick to gain our attention, a subtler variant on the "Proceed at your own risk" prologue that is the thrillseeker's welcome mat; but if that were the case there would be little purpose in reiterating the trick in the epilogue.

Besides stating that the story is and must be fiction, the epilogue invites the reader to take further advantage of this fact by choosing between several different endings. More precisely, it offers a choice of endings for George Smith, once Outerbridge and Quigley have been efficiently consigned to a happy and productive marriage. Regarding Smith, the reader is first told that he was treated and cured, married Anna, and inherited his aunt's farm, where he continues to live quietly and harmlessly. Then again, "if the idea of such as George still offends you, why it's the easiest thing in the world to have therapy fail and we'll wall him up forever"; and if even this does not suffice, he could be killed off in a riot or an escape attempt. The reader is even offered a choice of where he might be shot, based on Smith's own observation that in western films, "if the good guy gets shot it's always in the chest or shoulder and if the bad guy gets shot it's always in the belly."

A shot to the chest would mark Smith as a tragic hero, a shot to the belly would mark him as a bad guy; but morally speaking, *Some of Your Blood* is a somewhat trickier proposition than either the traditional western or the traditional vampire story. The mention of the belly echoes Anna's nickname for Smith, which is both a distortion of his real name and an unwitting insight into her lover's view of their relationship: as deduced by Quigley, "Rabbits and squirrels and little boys and old watchmen—each one is a mamma, full of warm sustaining fluid." In offering us the choice of having Smith shot in the belly, the narrator reminds us both of Anna's devotion to him and of the fact that his crimes derive from the appetites of a literally infantile part of his psyche. By implication, to want Smith shot in the belly is to want the shooting of a child, and a beloved child at that.

This ethical bait-and-switch is followed by the book's final paragraph: "But you'd better put the file back and clear out. If Dr. Outerbridge suddenly returns you'll have to admit he's real, and then all of this is. And that wouldn't do, would it?" This makes clear the reason behind the neurotic tone of those earlier reassurances: the case of George Smith may be fiction, but—unlike a fiction about a supernatural vampire—it could be real. Poverty and deprivation; drunken fathers and battered families; children whose home lives are so miserable that they find prison or the army not only tolerable but a genuine improvement; men who commit horrible crimes for reasons they themselves cannot understand: everything in the story could have happened and is always happening. It may be denied (it really is fiction) or dressed up as entertainment (you are the reader and it is your privilege); but manifestly it will not do.

About the Contributors

Michael J. Abolafia is a co-editor of *Dead Reckonings*.

Leigh Blackmore is an Australian horror writer, critic, editor, occultist, and musician. He was the Australian representative for the Horror Writers of America and served as the second president of the Australian Horror Writers Association.

Ramsey Campbell is an English horror fiction writer, editor, and critic who has been writing for well over fifty years. He is frequently cited as one of the leading writers in the field. His web- site is www.ramseycampbell.com.

Philip Challinor has published several articles on the work of Robert Aickman, some of which were collected in the chapbook *Akin to Poetry* (2010). He posts satire, fiction, and assorted grumbles on a blog, The Curmudgeon, and his longer fiction is available at Lulu.com.

Helen Chazan graduated with a degree in Classics. Her writing has previously appeared in several publications including *The Comics Journal* and *Dead Reckonings*.

Gary Fry lives in Dracula's Whitby, literally around the corner from where Bram Stoker was staying when he was thinking about that character. Gary has a Ph.D. in psychology, but his first love is literature. He is the author of many short story collections, novellas, and novels. He was the first author in PS Publishing's Showcase series, and none other than Ramsey Campbell has described him as "a master."

Fiona Maeve Geist lives with her cat in WXXT country, where she freelances RPGs and writes short fiction. Her work has appeared in *Lamplight Quarterly,* CLASH Media, *Mothership* (RPG), and *Ashes and Entropy*.

Edward Guimont recently received his Ph.D. from the University of Connecticut Department of History

Alex Houstoun is a co-editor of *Dead Reckonings*.

S. T. Joshi is the author of such critical studies as *The Weird Tale* (1990), *H. P. Lovecraft: The Decline of the West* (1990), and *Un- utterable Horror: A History of Supernatural Fiction* (2012). He has prepared corrected editions of H. P. Lovecraft's work for Arkham House and annotated editions of the weird tales of Lovecraft, Algernon Blackwood, Lord Dunsany, M. R. James, Arthur Machen, and Clark Ashton Smith for Penguin Classics, as well as the anthology *American Supernatural Tales* (2007).

Karen Joan Kohoutek, an independent scholar and poet, has published about weird fiction in various journals and literary websites. Recent and upcoming publications have been on subjects including the Gamera films, the Robert E. Howard/H. P. Lovecraft correspondence, folk magic in the novels of Ishmael Reed, and the proto-Gothic writer Charles Brockden Brown. She lives in Fargo, North Dakota.

Michael D. Miller is an adjunct professor and NEH medievalist summer scholar with numerous one-act play productions, awards, including several optioned screenplays to his credit, and authored the *Realms of Fantasy* RPG for Mythopoeia Games Publications. His poetry has appeared *Spectral Realms* and scholarly publications in *Lovecraft Annual*.

Daniel Pietersen is a writer of weird fiction and horror philosophy. He has a blog of fragmentary work and other thoughts at constantuniversity.wordpress.com.

Daniel Raskin lives in Minneapolis, where he performs noise electronics as *permanent waves* and aggravated anti-sociality as one half of the electro band *intercourse*. He is indebted to the web of friendship and collaboration which facilitates these and other pursuits.

Géza A. G. Reilly is a writer and critic with an interest in twentieth-century American genre literature. A Canadian expatriate, he now lives in the wilds of Florida with his wife, Andrea, and their cat, Mim.

Darrell Schweitzer is an American writer, editor, and critic in the field of speculative fiction. Much of his focus has been on dark fantasy and horror, although he does also work in science fiction and fantasy.

Donald Sidney-Fryer is a poet, historian, entertainer, and one of the foremost experts on the work of Clark Ashton Smith. His latest book, *A King Called Arthor and Other Morceaux,* was published by Hippocampus Press.

CPSIA information can be obtained
at www.ICGtesting.com
Printed in the USA
BVHW071018301020
592209BV00022B/1047

9 781614 983002